Reincarnation And Its Phenomena

'Who' or 'What' Becomes Reincarnated

Reincarnation And Its Phenomena
'Who' or 'What' Becomes Reincarnated

by

Filippo Liverziani

Regency Press (London & New York) Ltd.
125 High Holborn, London WC1V 6QA

ISBN 0 7212 0789 8

Printed and bound in Great Britain by
Buckland Press Ltd., Dover, Kent.

CONTENTS

CHAPTER I

The Problem: "Who" or "What" Becomes Reincarnated?

THE question posed in the title is one of the first that seems to come spontaneously to mind when one thinks about the idea of reincarnation. The answers that are traditionally given to this question can, to all intents and purposes, be reduced to two basic types.

1) It is "somebody," i.e. a certain *individuality*, that becomes reincarnated at successive moments in different *personalities*, each of which corresponds to a particular and distinct earthly existence.

2) What becomes reincarnated does not seem capable of being defined as a "somebody," but rather as a "something," as some psychic element; the nature of this element calls for further research, but it does not seem possible to identify it correctly or justifiedly with either a concrete personality, or with the essential nucleus of an individuality, or with what is commonly called a "soul."

By way of example, one may recall the summary definition of the term "reincarnation" given by Ian Stevenson, a well-known American scholar of phenomena of the reincarnation type: " . . . the union of a soul with a new physical body after the death of the physical body with which it had previously been associated."[1] Stevenson, who attributes this definition very broadly to the ambit of Hinduism, supplements it with another of what he feels should preferably be called *rebirth* rather than *reincarnation* and which he attributes, just as broadly speaking, to the general context of Buddhism: "rebirth is the activation of a new physical body by effects or residues that had previously been associated with another (now deceased) physical body."[2]

It is not easy to determine exactly what Buddha himself thought about this matter, and for our immediate purposes it is more interesting and relevant to refer to particular ideas that are widely held as part of historical Buddhism. After consulting a wide variety of texts, I prefer to continue at this point by quoting a statement made with admirable

clarity and concision by Radhakrishnan, an illustrious historian of
Indian philosophy: "There is no such thing in Buddhism as the
migration of the soul or the passage of an individual from life to life.
When a man dies his physical organism, which is the basis of his
psychical dissolves, and so the psychical life comes to an end. It is not
the dead man who comes to rebirth but another. There is no soul to
migrate. It is the character that continues."[3]

This character seems to form a single whole with the result of the
previous actions, with the fruit of these actions or *karman*. The karma
seems to be not only the active principle that brings about the rebirth
but, indeed, the very thing that is reborn. Consciousness, which at the
moment of death has its last refuge in the heart, continues to exist by
virtue of the karma and, under its impulsion, transfers itself into
another refuge created by this selfsame karma. There, according to the
words of Buddhagosa Visuddhimagga,[4] "the former consciousness,
from its passing out of existence, is called passing away, and the latter,
from its being reborn into a new existence, is called rebirth. But it is to
be understood that *this latter consciousness did not come to the
present existence from the previous one,* and also that it is only to
causes contained in the old existence, namely to karma or
predisposition, to inclination, . . . that its appearance is due."[5]

I should now like to compare these quotations with a passage to be
found in Vasubandhu's *Abhidharmakosha,* which many authoritative
scholars consider to be one of the books that best explain the
Buddhism of ancient times and bring out many of its innermost
implications.[6] Before I do so, let me give a definition of *skandha,* a
word that is going to crop up time and time again. According to a
canonical text, "the fardel is made up of the five skandhas: matter,
sensations, ideas, desires, knowledge; he who bears the fardel is the
pugdala, the person, for example, this venerable religious of such and
such a family, bearing such and such a name.[7]

Notwithstanding the actual words of the text I am about to quote,
this implies that the continuity of the person will never be completely
denied, just as in ancient Buddhism – no matter what some particular
sects may have held in this connection – there is no trace of any real
solution of continuity between one incarnation and the next.[8]

Having made these aspects clear, we can now take a look at the
passage from the *Abhidharmakosha:* "The heterodox, who believed in
the *atman,* says: 'If you admit that the being (*sattva*) goes into the

other world, the atman in which I believe is proven.' To confute this doctrine, the author says: The atman does not exist. The atman in which you believe, an entity that abandons the *skandhas* of one existence and takes the skandhas of another existence, an interior agent, a *Purusha*, such an atman does not exist. Bhagavat, in fact, has said: 'The act is; the fruit is; but there is no agent of any kind that abandons these skandhas and takes some other skandhas, independently of the causal relationship of the *dharma*.' What is this causal relationship? It can be expressed as follows: since this is, that is; from the birth of this, the birth of that (. . .). There is, then, asks the heterodox, a kind of atman that you do not deny? The skandhas, nothing else, conditioned by the passion and the act go to become reincarnated by means of the series of intermediate existence (. . .). We do not by any means deny an atman that exists by designation, an atman that is nothing other than a name given to the skandhas. But it is a far cry from this to the thought that the skandhas pass into the other world! They are momentary: they are incapable of transmigrating."[9]

Let us now go back to Radhakrishnan to see what appears to be his conclusion in this matter: "The man who is reborn is the heir of the action of the dead man. Yet he is a new being."[10] What survives is not the individual soul, but rather the *karman*. Radhakrishnan concludes; "the main tendency of Buddhism is to make karma the surviving element."[11]

The last of the factors of the personality (*skandhas*) "consciousness" (or *viññana*), which is the element that is really thought to transmigrate from one body into another, would really be better defined, as another author points out, as a "germ of consciousness" that is made up of "a life-craving set of character dispositions and latent memories which becomes attached to a new embryo to form a fresh empirical self. This system of dispositions corresponds roughly to the western concept of a 'psychic factor' and is, in eastern thought, viññana, 'that which rebecomes', not consciousness but rather a dispositional state, the karmic deposit of the past."[12]

I am not trying to establish here which particular tendency may be the one that predominates in Buddhism. All I want to do is to show that there are – and indeed always have been – many reincarnationists who deem that what is involved in transmigration is not the soul, not the nucleus of the individuality, but rather (and more limitedly) *something of a psychic nature*, something that formed part of this personality and subsequently became detached from it. If this is the idea of rebirth that prevails in Buddhism, one could deduce from it that its proponents constitute a strong minority among reincarnationists, for I quite agree that this is not the majority view; alternately, lest it be said that this minority is not even numerically strong, it is at least a highly qualified minority.(13)

At this point one might say that Buddhists (or, at least, a goodly number of Buddhists) arrive at this idea because their starting point, as is quite general in Buddhism and typical of it, is represented by their negation of the substantiality of the soul, by their denial that the soul can have any kind of substantiality (be this something of the soul's own or something it derives from God). I would reply to any objection of this kind by saying that what is of interest here is to show that the idea of reincarnation or transmigration or rebirth (or whatever else one may want to call it) as defined in the second of the two definitions given at the beginning is far removed from being an abstract or theoretical idea, but rather something that is concretely professed and lived by numerous people in the world or, at least, a certain number of rather well-qualified people. The theoretical foundation from which they deduce this idea is really the last thing that interests us here. When faced with such a widely accepted idea, it is surely far more interesting to see whether it can be referred to some spiritual experience. That something of a psychic nature becomes reincarnated may well have been experienced, and in a substantially concordant manner, by a multitude of different subjects through some form of clairvoyance, extrasensorial perception, spiritual sensitivity, or any other name one may give it.(14)

And for this reason, even if one were to feel bound to contest the theoretical premises underlying the structure of Buddhism, even if one felt bound to contest the general metaphysical perspective of Buddhism, this fact of experience could quite possibly be capable of being transferred into a different context, into a different metaphysical and religious perspective. And, if so, why not in a biblical, Christian, monotheist and humanist perspective (to roll them all into one)? But this is a problem that we can only set ourselves at a much later stage.

For the moment let us go back to the first of our two ideas of reincarnation, according to which the *quid* that becomes reincarnated is a subjectivity in the proper sense of the term, a soul, the core of an individuality. This is the idea currently professed by the large majority of reincarnationists. Ordinarily, this is precisely what is understood by the term "reincarnation". As we shall see more clearly later on, even Stevenson, when speaking of reincarnation and cases that suggest it, always has in mind a reincarnation phenomenon in the acceptance of the first of our two definitions.

The first text that expresses this reincarnation concept in a complete and extremely clear manner is the Fourth Brahmana of the Fourth Reading of the *Brhad-Aranyaka Upanishad*. Here I shall limit myself to quoting the initial passage of this text: "When that self becomes weak and unconscious, as it were, the organs gather around it. Having wholly seized these particles of light, the self comes to the heart.When the presiding deity of the eye turns back from all sides, the dying man fails to notice colour.

"The eye becomes united with the subtle body; then people say: 'He does not see'. The nose becomes united with the subtle body; then they say: 'He does not smell'. The tongue becomes united with the subtle body; then they say: 'He does not taste'. The vocal organ becomes united with the subtle body; then they say: 'He does not speak'. The ear becomes united with the subtle body: then they say: 'He does not hear'. The mind becomes united with the subtle body; then they say: 'He does not think'. The skin becomes united with the subtle body; then they say: 'He does not touch'. The intellect becomes united with the subtle body; then they say: 'He does not know'. The upper end of the heart lights up, and by that light the self departs, either through the eye or through the head or through any other aperture of the body. And when the self departs, the vital breath follows, and when the vital breath departs, all the organs follow. Then the self becomes endowed with specific consciousness and passes on to the body to be attained by that consciousness. Knowledge, work, and past experience follow the self.

"And just as a leech moving on a blade of grass reaches its end, takes hold of another, and draws itself together towards it, so does the self, after throwing off this body, that is to say, after making it unconscious, take hold of another support and draw itself together towards it."

Koshelya Walli, an Indian scholar and author of a book about the doctrine of the karma in Indian thought,[16] notes that in this *upanishad* "we have a clear statement that the soul leaves one body and enters into another."[17] That "the soul assumes a body due to its past karma, as Walli goes on to say, is one of the notions which "in India we generally believe," it is one of the ideas that "reflect the usual trend of Indian thought, though in one of its features only."[18]

According to this idea, which seems to be far and away the most widely held among reincarnationists, be they Indian or non-Indian, eastern or western, it is a certain individuality that becomes reincarnated: it is a certain individuality that has to become reincarnated, or stands in need of, endeavours to, or is in some way involved in becoming reincarnated, in order to be able to have certain experiences. But, as one may ask, for what reason? Many different motivations can be suggested in answer to this question: expiating some fault, purifying itself, making certain kinds of new experiences for its own spiritual development, or even satisfying some caprice or giving expression to some impulse of passion or – gradually rising to higher levels – giving vent to ambitions, exercising talents, fulfilling missions.

It is well known, moreover, that believers in transmigration of the soul also seek to insert reincarnation in a theoretical and doctrinal framework: reincarnation, they generally say, is the only thing capable of explaining the reality of evil and disparity among men, the only thing that can explain why some men are fortunate and blessed with talents, while others seem less favoured by fate, less evolved and less capable of evolution, sometimes tainted psychically with predispositions that compel them to act in an immoral and even criminal manner, placed at a disadvantage in many different ways, or condemned to suffer far more than others.

However one views it, reincarnation is always seen as involving a soul, an individual that desires or has to become reincarnated in a particular condition either because he merits such reincarnation or because he has to undergo some punishment or to purify himself, and so on. What becomes reincarnated is always a subject in the sense of the first definition, i.e. a subject that survives because he has a permanent essence of his own and therefore does not merely survive but is, indeed, immortal.

At this point there arises the problem of trying to see whether such a "substantiality" of the human subject finds some confirmation in experience. As we shall see in Chapter V, Emilio Servadio, to name but one, denies this: what we learn to know in the course of experience is our empirical ego; but – either for pathological reasons or even as a result of simple ageing – our "sense of the ego" can undergo an infinite range of modifications, distortions, or diminutions. Even psychoanalysis itself shows us that the life of the ego is characterized by a situation of continuous dependence, weakness, variability, instability. What, indeed, is there in our empirical ego that is truly substantial and authorizes us to identify it with the "soul" that is thought to survive and to become reincarnated, maintaining a continuous or, rather, perennial identity with itself?

It is quite true that this problem could be reformulated in somewhat different terms. Even if it were to be admitted that there are no elements that enable us to affirm the reality of a substantial ego as such, an originary substantial ego on its own account, there still remains an open problem that could be stated more or less as follows: whether or not, though devoid of an originary substantiality of its own, the ego could possess a substantiality that derives from God. In that case the empirical ego would derive its substantiality solely and exclusively from the fact that God himself is present deep down in the intimacy of this ego, and is present there in a very particular manner. Seen in this perspective, man here on earth would be a privileged dwelling-place of divine presence and manifestation. This is the perspective of a God who creates man in his image and likeness, and even incarnates himself in this man, so that each one of us might become a tiny potential absolute, something lofty in a horizon of infinite possibilities that include, for each one of us, personal immortality. This is the perspective of a human kind not only substantial and immortal but potentially infinite, and this not *in se* or by its own merits, but rather as the derivation of a divine Source that springs deep down within each one of us and is more intimately "us" than our own self.

How could a perspective of this kind be convalidated? Certainly not as a result of scientific proof, but rather and exclusively through the deepening of a certain type of religious experience. As things stand today, we are here clearly concerned with something that is not equally within reach of us all, because each one of us carries within him a different degree of maturation. It is therefore a perspective that, as far as our immediate purposes are concerned, we can do no more than mention very briefly as a possible reference point, as a possibility of salvation for a human individuality that would otherwise seem wholly labile and ephemeral.

If we want to maintain our discussion at levels that seem capable of a more objective approach, it seems desirable, at least at the beginning, to ask ourselves to what extent we may be justified in speaking of an individuality that becomes reincarnated and yet maintains itself one and the same all the time, a determined and substantial individuality that remains coherent with itself, somewhat in the manner of the string of a pearl necklace that, behind the outward dissimilarity of the individual pearls, maintains its unity in continuity with itself. In that case our terms of reference can be nothing other than the facts, that is to say, the sum total of all the phenomena that suggest reincarnation. We have to take a close look to see whether and to what extent the various phenomena of the reincarnation type confirm the reality of a reincarnation conceived on the model of our first definition.

But even if this model were to enter into crisis and become untenable, this would not automatically mean that we would have to exclude all possibility of reincarnation, no matter how it might be conceived; indeed, if an examination of these phenomena were to lead us to conclude that there nevertheless exists some form of reincarnation, we would still have to consider the model deriving from our second definition.

And there we would have to ask ourselves whether this model is necessarily bound up with a Buddhist perspective or, alternatively, whether it could be integrated into a different perspective and outlook. Indeed, it may well be that such a different perspective could be given a better foundation, a greater and deeper "content of truth". But these are problems that we should not pose ourselves until a much later stage, because it is best to take things in order and to proceed step by step.

CHAPTER II

Hypnotic Regression to "Previous Lives"

IN any kind of scientific investigation, it is always a good idea to divide the difficulties and to begin with the less difficult things, concentrating attention initially on matters that seem relatively simple and more obvious. The phenomena that suggest reincarnation seem to be capable of being divided into two broad categories, namely *spontaneous phenomena* and *artificially provoked phenomena,* the latter produced mainly by means of hypnotic regression or, as it is more commonly referred to, *age regression.* Indeed, age regression can be pushed to the period that precedes birth and, going even further, to times prior to conception and eventually also to presumed previous incarnations.

Among these two groups of phenomena that suggest reincarnation, as we shall later see, the provoked phenomena involve a much smaller degree of difficulty than the spontaneous ones and this has induced me to consider them first. We shall thus leave the spontaneous phenomena until a later stage, because these have to be considered with particular attention and seem to call for an interpretation that is far more complex than either the common form of reincarnationism in accordance with the first definition of Chapter I or – to go to the other extreme – its simple negation.

The range of provoked phenomena is very considerable and includes those that emerge from experiments carried out with the help of such hypnagogic drugs as mescaline, psilocybin and lysergic acid (LSD). The use of any one of these hallucinogenous drugs, in appropriate doses and under medical supervision of course, will induce an altered state of consciousness in the subject that normally lasts for several hours. In the course of treatments of this kind the patient can have sensations and visions connected with past experiences, even with experience of birth or of previous lives. However, material of this type is as yet rather scarce, while reports about hypnotic regressions are available with a certain abundance. Let us therefore concentrate our attention on the later, which we may regard as the paradigm of provoked phenomena that suggest reincarnation.

In hypnotic regression the experimenter causes the subject to fall into a hypnotic trance either by means of magnetic passes (following Mesmer's original method: and here we have classical *Mesmerism*) or by means of suggestion (in which case we have *hypnotism* in the strict sense of the term). Mesmer was convinced that hypnosis was brought about by a magnetic force (animal magnetism) that flowed forth from the hands of the "magnetizer" and became communicated to the subject by means of the passes, although later it was realized that the essential factor was suggestion and that the passes could represent a ceremonial (essential, I would say, but not always sufficient) act to produce this suggestion. It is then suggested to the hypnotized subject that he or she should go back to the time when, let us say, he was ten years of age or even younger; this is followed by similar suggestions to return first to the time when he was still in his mother's womb, subsequently to his previous incarnation and then, step by step, to other incarnations in even more remote periods of time.

Let us see what can happen in such experiments. A seventeen-year-old girl hypnotized by Dr. Pitre of the Medical Faculty of Bordeaux University, on being taken back to the age of five, no longer understands when spoken to in French but, by way of compensation as it were, remembers and begins to express herself in the Gascon dialect she had spoken as a small child and subsequently forgotten.[19] Or, as in the case of a very poor German woman from Bad Homburg taken right back to a previous existence, it can happen that the subject begins to speak in perfect French, a language she had never known or learnt in her "German" life. This woman told Prince Galitzin, the hypnotizer, that her present unhappy life was the punishment for having killed her husband in a previous one by pushing him off a cliff in order to be able to marry her lover. Prince Galitzin and his collaborator in the experiment went to check the story and had it confirmed by some old peasants who, from their own parents, had heard the story of a beautiful young woman suspected of having killed her husband in that manner. All the details mentioned by the hypnotized subject fitted perfectly with the locally known facts. The police station at Bad Homburg further confirmed that the woman, a prostitute of the lowest order, had never had any education and was quite unable to speak French.[20]

Hypnotic experiments of this type are particularly associated with the name of Eugène De Rochas (1837-1914). But for the moment let us concentrate our attention on *age regressions* and *regressions to previous lives* (or presumed to be such) like those practiced by Morey Bernstein, an American amateur hypnotist whose name is associated with the famous "Bridey Murphy" case, and by Thorwald Dethlefsen, an equally well-known German psychotherapist and hypnotist. Bernstein defines age repression as "the ability of the subject, while under hypnosis, to relive or recall detailed incidents of the past, even though such incidents may have taken place during infancy."[21] Bernstein also makes a distinction between a certain type of regression, where the subject recounts an experience as if he were watching it, and another, which he calls "authentic or total regression", where the subject seems effectively to be reliving a past episode in the first person.

Dethlefsen, on the other hand, speaks of age regression as a "method capable of taking persons under hypnosis back to a previous age in life."[22] He stresses that what is at stake in true age regression is not so much making the subject *remember* certain episodes far removed in time, but rather causing him to *relive* them.

More substantially, Bernstein gets his subjects to lie down on a couch and to fix their eyes on a lit candle, suggesting to them that they should let themselves go and sink into an ever deeper hypnotic sleep. Let us now see, albeit very summarily, what happened during the course of a session he began at 10.35 p.m. on 29th November 1952, when the subject was Mrs. Virginia Tighe, aged twenty-nine, referred to in his book under the pseudonym "Ruth Simmons". No sooner had a sufficient degree of trance been attained than Bernstein turned to "Ruth" with the following suggestion: "When I talk to you next, you will be seven years old, and you can answer my questions. Now. Now, you are seven years old."[23] In answer to specific questions, little by little, "Ruth" supplied the name of her school, the names of some of the boys and girls in her class, and other information about what she was doing at the time.

After a moment's rest, Bernstein then says to his subject (and henceforth I shall use only the present tense in relating these experiments): "We're going to turn even farther back through space and time. we're going back now to the time when you were five years old."[24] And now the woman regressed to being a little girl, continuing to answer Bernstein's questions, speaks of the kindergarten she is attending, of her world and the other children, her toys, and so on. Then, using the same system and with the same questions and answers, "Ruth" is made to regress to three years of age, and subsequently to being a baby girl just one year old.

At this point she is urged to regress even further, Bernstein using the following words: "I want you to keep on going back and back in your mind. And, surprising as it may seem, strange as it may seem, you will find that there are other scenes in your memory. There are other scenes from faraway lands and distant places in your memory. I will talk to you again. I will talk to you again in a little while. I will talk to you again in a little while. Meanwhile your mind will be going back, back, back, and back until it picks up a scene, until, oddly enough, you find yourself in some other scene, in some other place, in some other time, and when I talk to you again you will tell me about it."[25]

At this point, albeit after a further pause, the hypnotist asks his subject very firmly: "What have you seen?" And here are the answers given by "Ruth", haltingly at first, then with ever increasing sureness: "... Uh ... scratched the paint off all my bed. Jus' painted it, 'n' made it pretty. It was a metal bed, and I scratched the paint off of it. Dug my nails on every post and just ruined it. Was just terrible." Bernstein comes in: "Why did you do that?" "Don't know. I was just mad. Got an awful spanking." "What is your name?" "... Uh ... Friday."[26] This name, at first perceived in this manner, is then specified more clearly: not "Friday", but "Bridey". And the surname of this new personage is "Murphy", an Irish lassie, four years of age on the occasion of the first regression, living in Cork, with her family, which she describes in a certain manner, and the year is ... 1806. Little by little, a lot of other detailed information is then provided. Both in the first session and in subsequent ones the personality of Bridey Murphy thus begins to take ever clearer shape, just as her biography emerges and becomes gradually denser as regressions interplay with progressions. She is the daughter of Duncan Murphy, a Protestant lawyer, while her mother is called Kathleen and her elder brother Duncan. The family lives just outside Cork, at a place called "The Meadows". At the age of twenty Bridey marries Brian MacCarthy (a Catholic, a lawyer like her father, and later lecturer at Queen's University), moves to Belfast, where she spends the rest of her life, eventually dying there in 1864. Obviously, I can't give all the details here.

In a case like that of Bridey Murphy, where a great many items of information are interconnected to form a pattern that, at least at first sight, seems plausible, the best thing to do is probably to suspend judgment until such time as one can see whether and to what extent this information can be verified. However, because in considering cases of hypnotic regression to hypothetical previous lives it is always a good to begin with something that is relatively easy and presents a minimum of difficulties, I should first like to consider another case reported by Dethlefsen.

On 3rd June 1968, in fact, Dethlefsen and a number of acquaintances met at a house in Munich for a collective hypnotic experiment, in the course of which he obtained the most conspicuous results with a student, twenty-five years of age, referred to as Rudolf T. On being caused to regress to the age of six, then four and two, and eventually to the moment of his birth, the young man, breathing with difficulty, described his dominant impression with the following words: "It's light and cold."[27] But the hypnotist keeps on suggesting: "Let's go back a little further, to just before your birth . . . What do you feel, what is your impression?" "It's a little tight". "Can you see something?" "No." "Let's go back another two months! Tell me, what do you feel?" "Nothing, nothing!" "Let's go back even further, a whole year! Where are you now?" "I don't know!" "Is it light or dark?" "I can't see anything, it is all so empty!" "Tell me your name!" "I have no name!" "What year is it?" "I don't know!"[28] At this stage Dethlefsen keeps pressing with his suggestions, trying to provoke a further regression: "Let's go back, back, back, until you come up against some salient event that you manage to describe in words!" And Rudolf T., still breathing in spurts and with difficulty, suddenly tells him: "I'm in a cellar." "Where is the cellar, in what place, which city?" "Wissembourg." "What country are you in?" "In France." "What is your name?" "Guy Lafarge." "Where are you?" "In a cellar." "What road is the cellar in?" "Rue du Connétable!" "Why are you in the cellar?" "War." "Is it wartime?" "Yes." "Which war?" "Against the Prussians." "What year is it?" "1870." "How old are you then?" "Eighteen!"[29]

In the course of this first hypnotic session, as during the second held a week later, the subject supplied further information, though on the

whole considerably less detailed than the biography adduced by
"Bridey Murphy". On Dethlefsen's specific invitation, Rudolf T. says a
few simple phrases in French, gets a couple of dates wrong (perhaps
excusably so, seeing that the hypnotist keeps on marching him forward
and backward in time) and, lastly, when still in the years around 1870,
places a "King Louis" at the head of the French state.

In this case, as in most others, Dethlefsen gives us no case history
whatsoever, does not provide us with even a minimum of information
about the subject or his level of education and knowledge or, more
generally, about his cultural background (although this would seem to
have been above the average of Dethlefsen's subjects).

Since we are concerned with a twenty-five-year old student, at
university level, one may presume that he must have studied French at
school, though without taking any great interest in French history and
her domestic politics, being quite satisfied with a few general notions
about Prussian victories that, like all German schoolboys, he would
have picked up long, long ago from some manual or textbook. In fact,
at Wissembourg (which was not by any means a village of 250 people,
as the subject tells us, but rather a fully fledged little town and
administrative headquarters of the district) a French division was
annihilated by the Prussians on 4th August, 1870.

Another case included in Dethlefsen's book, called *Life after Life,* is
that of Klaus-Peter S., born in 1954, who, after being regressed to
1897, claimed to be a certain Jean Dupré, son of an otherwise
unidentified baron. The subject talks about his home in Paris, though it
is not really clear whether this is a castle or a mansion, does not speak
a word of French and, on being asked to explain this, is at a complete
loss. He seems to know nothing about the city other than that it is
traversed by the Seine and that the church of Notre Dame rises there
(two very obvious points), telling us also that the throne was occupied
by a "Sun King" (which, bearing in mind that we are at the end of the
nineteenth century, is even more incorrect than the King Louis of
whom Guy Lafarge deemed himself to be a subject).

The author seems to derive an exaggerated satisfaction from the
results of these "regressions". Indeed, the revelations about previous
lives that emerge from them (and which are really no more than
presumed and remain wholly to be demonstrated) constitute reasons for
astonishment and even shock as far as he is concerned. It is quite true
that when he asks a hypnotized subject to write his name after having

been regressed, successively to 18, 15, 12, 10, 8, 7 and 6 years of age, the published signatures seem to become, at least in general appearance, gradually more infantile; but Dethlefsen does not tell us whether he tried to obtain control specimens in the form of real samples of the subject's handwriting in childhood preserved by him as keepsakes. He does not even tell us whether the subject had some knowledge of French or whether he subjected him to some cultural or psychological test to see whether and to what extent his revelations about his previous lives, can or cannot be attributed to the mental patrimony associated with his present-day personality.

And what should we say about a subsequent book by the same author, published under the title *Experience of Reincarnation?*[30] Apart from certain considerations made in this book, and I shall come back to these a little later, it seems to me that the answers given by Dethlefsen's hypnotized patients do not really yield much more than we have already seen. It is quite true that the revelations, such as they are, are often confirmed after a certain lapse of time in response to questions formulated in a completely different manner, but it is equally true that these answers remain extremely scanty, devoid of any verification in historical reality, and often of such a nature as to produce a rather strange effect on readers that are not wholly on the level of the uneducated.

As regards the lack of historical confirmation, let me be quite truthful and say that there is one exception: a female subject, a journalist by profession, was regressed to a presumed previous life as Anna Schwenzer, born on 17th April, 1832 at Neuenbroock; subsequently, the lady journalist herself set out to make some diligent inquiries and discovered that an Anna Schwenzer, born in that place and on that exact day, had effectively existed. Another possible verification concerns the same subject, but this time in an anterior incarnation, because we are now back in 1580 and in the castle of the Strachwitz family on the banks of the Vltava, about six hours by coach from Prague: these are facts sufficiently within reach of anybody who really wants to verify them. And yet the only information that can be had is that surviving members of the Strachwitz family claim that the family comes from that part of Bohemia, "even though there are no documents relating to this period."[31] This, surely, is very strange for a family that possessed such a clearly identifiable castle in a period that, when all is said and done, is not all that far removed from our own days. The contents that the various subjects bring out, a little at a time, arouse a continuous impression of approximation, and the subjective nature of their statements becomes even more evident when they say things that are altogether unreal and devoid of any possible verification, if not false in the fullest sense of the term. Here one need only think, to give but two examples, of the English personage that in the first half of the eighteenth century keeps on saying O.K. at every possible occasion (as a synonym for "right" or "all right") when it is well known that this expression first came into use in the United States in year 1840;[32] or of the poor Natasha, born in 1851 as the daughter of a Russian grand duke, fully convinced that her father's grand duchy, far from being a merely honorary title, corresponded to a kind of kingdom, a sovereign state.[33]

Incongruencies of this kind do not seem to attract the attention of our hypnotherapist even at a later stage, when he sits down to transcribe the answers given by his subjects and to publish them word by word. He does, quite honestly, confess to be "highly ignorant" in history,[34] but he should also recognize that, in the absence of any interdisciplinary collaboration with specialists in historical research, it is precisely his complete lack of preparation in this field that puts him in a far from ideal position for ascertaining that what his subjects (at least those he tells us about) are testifying has very little to do with history. His experiments are devoid of control and not even subjected to critical remarks; all one finds is an attitude of marvelling conviction that in no manner contradicts his erstwhile enthusiasm, almost as if the author were telling us every now and again: "Just listen to this, isn't it marvellous?"

Before anything that emerges from such regressions can be taken into consideration as something more than a pure and simple psychological phenomenon, as something that in one way or another brings us face to face with the problem of reincarnation, it is quite essential that what is said should correspond to some objective fact, to historical data or recorded events. Frederick Lenz, in his book *Lifetimes, True Accounts of Reincarnation*,[35] dedicates an entire paragraph, about twenty pages long and entitled "Confirmation", to this particular aspect; and he was there concerned with memories that emerged spontaneously in the subjects, just as in the cases studied by Stevenson, which we shall consider later. In this book, as also in Stevenson's researches, we have a serious attempt to ascertain, always within the limits of the possible, whether the "remembered" facts had really happened. But books with such titles as *Life after Life, Life before Life, Experience of Reincarnation, You Have Been Here Before* etc., simply entrust the convalidation of the theses they put forward so radically (and clamorously) in the titles to nothing other than the tales of past lives told with details that would cause any reader not altogether devoid of historical culture to bend with laughter and merriment, while a psychologist relates them without even raising an eyebrow. How is this possible? True, a psychologist, a hypnotherapist has his job to do and is not a professor of history, but one may at least ask what authorizes him to report so many blunders and obvious absurdities under such high-sounding titles. When faced with these obvious rehashes of a historical culture formed on the basis of television serials and pseudohistorical films of the worst kind, how is it that authors, whom the title pages of their books proudly announce with long strings of academic letters behind their names, do not assume even that modicum of critical attitude normally induced by no more than a minimum of general culture that, surely, one may presume holders of such high academic qualifications to possess?

As compared with the utter inconsistency of the data and information supplied by many of the subjects regressed by Dethlefsen, Edith Fiore, Helen Wambach, etc., we find an incomparably greater accuracy and wealth of detail in the "Bridey Murphy" case studied by Morey Bernstein. So much so that in his book entitled *Reincarnation? The Claims Investigated*, a careful review of some of the best known cases suggestive of reincarnation, Ian Wilson recognizes and admits Bridey Murphy's "consistent Irish brogue, her use of strange Irish words, her wealth of factual information about nineteenth-century Ireland, and her totally plausible life histories of ordinary people of the period."[36] It is an unfortunate fact, however, that births, deaths and marriages were not officially registered in Ireland prior to 1864 and it has not therefore proved possible to find any trace of either Bridey Murphy, her parents or her husband, just as there exists no record of a Dooley Road in nineteenth-century Belfast or, for that matter, of a Church of Saint Theresa, which in actual fact was constructed only as recently as 1901. These perplexities only increased when it was later discovered that Virginia Tighe had had an Irish aunt, who (though born in the United States) used to tell her stories about the Ireland of former days when she was a little girl. Another and even more disconcerting discovery came when it was found out that on the opposite side of the street, in which Virginia Tighe had her home in Chicago, there lived a certain Mrs. Bridey Murphy Corkell, a native of County Mayo, in Ireland. When Virginia was questioned about this, she promptly admitted that she knew this lady and also John "Buddy" Corkell, her son.

The Bridey Murphy case became very controversial and two leading Chicago newspapers took up the cudgels, one for and one against, no holds barred. The subject, who appeared to have no recollection whatsoever of anything she might have said under hypnosis, at times used wholly convincing Irish turns of phrase when in this condition, though at others she had recourse to Americanisms of obviously more modern origin. For a whole series of reasons and notwithstanding all the accusations of deceit that have been levelled against it, the Bridey Murphy case seems to be long-lived. As Wilson concludes, it can be adduced as proof of reincarnation only in a highly acritical manner, and yet it leaves an open problem, for it seems to express a certain "something", some phenomenon that is not by any means clear and still stands in need of explanation.[37]

Wilson also notes the great increase in the number of hypnotic regressions in the twenty-five years following Bernstein's experiments with Virginia Tighe. He makes particular mention of the experiments carried out by Arnall Bloxham of Cardiff, South Wales, and Joe Keeton of Hoylake, near Liverpool. Here I shall limit myself to quoting a few facts or comments from Wilson's analysis that seem to be of particular interest.

Keeton is convinced that there is no interval at all between one life and the next and his subjects reincarnate immediately, but this not in the sense of an immediate rebirth (as is the Druse view of reincarnation), but rather in the sense that they are immediately reconceived as a result of sexual union between their new parents (a view of reincarnation held among the Jains in Upper Burma).[38] If a subject does not reincarnate in exactly this manner, Keeton stops the treatment.[39] May I briefly point out here that, since the subjects presumably desire – at least subconsciously – to be taken into consideration by the hypnotist, this fact may well explain why the subjects Keeton investigates all become reincarnated according to this particular pattern. In marked contrast, however, Bloxham's subjects grant themselves rest periods in the astral spheres, sometimes even of considerable length, between one life and the next.[40]

In the case of one of Bloxham's subjects Wilson notes that his presumed description of the Vikings landing on the North American coast is more in line with current popular ideas of the Vikings than with the more accurate results of historical and archeological research: in fact, the characteristic helmets of these Scandinavian warriors were normally devoid of the horns with which they are consistently depicted in the drawings of schoolchildren, who draw their inspiration from boys' books and comic strips.[41]

Another observation made by Wilson, and a very pertinent one it seems to me, concerns the manner, the style with which these presumed personages of bygone times generally express themselves, for this style and choice of words seem to be more in line with novels, films and television serials devoted to historical topics than with the way people actually behaved and spoke at that particular time.[42]

More convincing seems to be the account given by Jane Evans, a pseudonym for another of Bloxham's subjects, of a massacre of Jews at York in 1190, an occasion when Jane was Rebecca.[43] Although inexactitudes and reasons for uncertainty abound, the general lines of the episode related by the subject correspond to historical reality. But the event constitutes a fairly well known historical fact, and Wilson wonders whether we can really be sure that the subject had not learnt anything about the massacre at the tower, possibly from books read and then forgotten, yet with the contents recorded in her unconscious memory. Unfortunately, we know too little about the subject, identified only by a pseudonym, to exclude this possibility.

But in the case of Alfred Orriss, regressed by Derek Crussel to the time of the Napoleonic wars, we do know that the subject took delight in reading about this period and that he had lived in Essex. This could explain why, on being regressed to his previous incarnation as a soldier of the 44th East Essex Regiment, the information of a general nature supplied by him was as accurate as that about his immediate superiors proved doubtful or altogether incorrect; indeed, patient research has revealed no trace of these names, even though appropriate documentation is available.[44]

A very positive impression is often made by the vivacity of the accounts, the dramatic manner in which some of these presumedly reincarnated personalities express themselves, the propriety of their speech, their pronunciation, especially of certain words that later underwent changes, and so on. But in all these cases, always provided we want to consider the possibility these previous incarnations are but projections of the subject's present personality, one should really set out to discover in what manner the subject may have learnt certain things in the course of his present existence (that, quite possibly, subsequently faded from his conscious recollection).

Some experiments carried out by Dr. Reima Kampman of Oulu University in Finland are particularly instructive in this connection. One example will be quite sufficient for our immediate purposes. More than ten years ago, Dr. Kampman hypnotized a young girl then attending secondary school and referred to as Niki (a pseudonym): regression produced a series of previous existences, including those lived as Karin Bergstrom (1932-39, a Finnish girl killed during an air raid), Dorothy (13th century, an English girl and daughter of an innkeeper), and Ving Lei (round about 100 a.d., a blind Chinese girl who died by falling from a cliff). Desiring to take a closer look at the most recent of these reincarnations, Kampman at a certain point hypnotized Niki again and then, rather then regressing her to previous lives, took her back to the precise moment at which she had first received the information that subsequently re-emerged in the form of the supposed reincarnation memories of the personality of Karin Bergstrom. And immediately Niki went back to a moment when she was perusing a book of photographs about Finland during the Second World War. One of the photographs bore the very address that Niki had given under hypnosis as the home of Karin Bergstrom and, right next to it, there was the photograph of a seven-year-old girl who, together with her mother, had died during an aerial bombardment on the very day that Niki had mentioned. Note, however, that the name of this girl was not Karin Bergstrom.

Using the same approach, Reima Kampman also identified the materials present in Niki's memory that had given rise to the personalities of Dorothy and Ving Lei. As far as Dorothy is concerned, Niki had at some time sung a "Summer Song" in slightly modernized medieval English and Dr. Kampman began to wonder about the source from which this came. When hypnotically regressed to the moment when she had first learnt this song, Niki revealed that she had read it – not without difficulty – in a book by Benjamin Britten and Imogen Holst entitled *The Phases of Music* or, in Finnish, *Musikiin Vaiheet*. She even remembered the page on which the song was printed, and it was all found to be exactly as she said.[45]

What we have just seen in Niki's case can be usefully compared with the findings of analogous investigations that Ian Wilson reports in Chapter VII of his book. Particularly worthy of mention here is an experiment carried out by Dr. Harold Rosen of Toronto, Canada, in the course of which one of his hypnotized patients wrote a text in a strange language that was subsequently identified as Oscan, an ancient Italic language. The text in question was the "Curse of Vibia", and Dr. Rosen eventually discovered that many years before, in the reading room of a library, his subject had been sitting next to another reader and had seen a reproduction of the curse in the Oscan original in a book that his neighbour had open in front of him. The patient had thus memorized the text at the level of his unconscious by mere virtue of the fact of having casually glanced at it, so much so that the version he produced under hypnosis many years later was substantially correct.[46]

It would seem that in our unconscious we retain, or are capable of retaining, extremely detailed memories even of things to which, consciously, we pay little or no attention. It is quite sufficient for these things to have passed before our eyes, to have been perceived in some way or other. Wilson reports a striking example of this type. On 18th July 1976 a hand-made bomb exploded in a bus on its way to Tel Aviv, Israel. The driver was among the unwounded survivors, but so many people had boarded the bus (and most of them had got off again a few stops later) that he could provide little or no useful information for the purpose of identifying the perpetrator of the attack. He eventually agreed to be hypnotized and proved to be a good subject as regards "reliving" his memories and impressions of the trip: regressed to the moment of departure, this subject described, among others, a dark-skinned young man who had got on with a parcel under his arm, bought his ticket from the driver, and had then left the bus a little while later. After being woken up, the driver was able to give such a clear description of this young man, right down to details of his clothing, that it proved possible to identify and arrest the presumed terrorist, who ended up by making a full confession.[47]

As we can see, the human mind is capable of preserving an exact and highly detailed record of things that have in passing been seen or even only glimpsed in passing, and it can do likewise with things that have been read or perused, albeit in a quite distracted fashion. When faced with regressions to presumed previous incarnations, one cannot dismiss that these previous "personalities" are not in some way constructed from elements that already form part of the subject's cultural baggage, part of his interior world, things that were learnt or absorbed at some moment of his present existence and subsequently disappeared from his conscious recollection, possibly because his attention was never focused on them. Not even the subject himself could really exclude this possibility, for his conscious memory, limited as it is to things that were learnt in a purposeful and concentrated manner, would be anything but a reliable witness in this matter.

No matter what the form of the original input, no matter whether we are concerned with things that have been seen or glimpsed, with pages that have been read or merely perused in haste, with hypnotic suggestion or auto-suggestion, the data and images involved are processed by the unconscious in a very complex manner, so much so as to provide the material for scenes, events and stories that the subject can relive in an extremely vivacious and even dramatic manner, often recounting in a highly articulate and colourful right manner down to the least detail.

Wilson also speaks of another very significant experiment made by Professor Ernest Hilgard, an eminent American psychologist who teaches at Stanford University. One of his students agreed to be hypnotized and regressed and thus found himself, somewhat unexpectedly perhaps, in Victorian England round about the middle of last century. To everybody's surprise, himself included, the subject began to speak about the royal family in the terms of absolute familiarity in which a contemporary would express himself. It was not difficult to check that what he was saying about the various members of the family and their relationships to each other was perfectly correct and hard historical fact. Speaking to Professor Hilgard the next day, the student revealed himself to be fully convinced that this was a case of reincarnation and readily offered him his collaboration for the purposes of a more thorough study of the phenomenon. Hilgard subsequently questioned the subject with great delicacy and ability in order to ascertain whether under hypnosis he could possibly have re-evoked memories of things that he had learnt during his present existence. In the end he thus came to discover that many years earlier the student had done a great deal of reading about the family of Queen Victoria and her husband and that later, having decided to dedicate himself to scientific studies, he had dropped his historical and literary interests, eventually forgetting all about his earlier readings and the things he had learnt through them. Indeed, it was only Hilgard's acute questioning that brought them back into his conscious recollection.

Hilgard realized that the only way he could convince the student of the pseudo-reincarnative character of his experience was to rehypnotise him and then induce him to relive in an analogous manner some wholly imaginary event that would be suggested to him in this state. As soon as the student had fallen into a deep trance, Hilgard suggested to him that he should take himself into a very specific situation, namely a place where, together with some friends, he had discovered an underground cavern that they were about to explore. As soon as he had received this suggestion, the subject launched himself into a most lively account of how he and his friends had organized and made the excursion, describing with a wealth of detail the place they had reached, the great rock they had climbed, the picnic at the top and the tunnel into which they had penetrated with the help of ropes and flashlights. This was followed by an equally detailed description of the cavern itself with all its stalagtites and stalagmites, a small underground lake, and the fantastic optical effects that were produced there. At a certain point, moreover, one of the young explorers discovers a second tunnel, this time very low and narrow, that requires them to proceed on all fours, one behind the other, until they suddenly emerge into a kind of Shangri-La, a marvellous valley described in equally vivacious detail by the student. When the subject was eventually woken up, he still remembered everything he had recounted and explained that he had experienced it all in an extremely lively fashion, just as if it were happening quite independently of his will and imagination, as if he were a spectator of real events.

In other words, everything was happening as if the subject under hypnosis had become divided into two distinct personalities: a kind of stage director, hidden in the wings of the subject's subconscious, was seemingly arranging and directing the events that, at the higher level of consciousness, the hypnotized student was to live and experience as a spectator, wholly unaware that he himself was ultimately writing the script, directing the plot as it were.[48] In a somewhat similar manner, even though most writers, poets, musicians, artists, and so on, produce their works at a more conscious level, sitting at a table perhaps, there are also many others who work out the substance of their creations, sometimes even down to minute details, at the level of the subconscious, whence they suddenly emerge at the most unexpected moments in more or less finished form.[49]

A noteworthy feature of all these phantasies is represented by the consistency of the individual elements, which as a general rule seem to fit together in perfectly logical fashion, each element harmonizing with the next as if there had been a conscious mind to select them in groups and to combine them in that particular fashion.

Wilson also shows rather clearly that the mechanism that seems to generate the various personalities of the supposed previous incarnations is ultimately not very different from the one underlying the phenomenon of alternating personalities.

Emilio Servadio, for example, defines this phenomenon as "consisting of the spontaneous and sudden alternation of two or more seemingly different personalities in one and the same individual" and stresses that each one of these personalities is perfectly coherent with itself, saying that ". . . there can be no doubt that *coherent patterns of thought and behaviour* can alternate in an exceptional manner in one and the same individual, so much so as to give the impression that on each occasion one is face to face with different personalities and sometimes even finds it difficult to decide which is the 'true' one, that is to say, the personality that would remain if one were to succeed in neutralizing the others or causing them to disappear."[50]

By way of example of the phenomenon of multiple personalities, we may here briefly consider the famous case of Chris Sizemore treated by two American psychiatrists, Corbett Thigpen of Augusta (Georgia) and Tony Tsitos of Annandale (Virginia), a case that provided the material first for a book that became a bestseller under the title of *The Three Faces of Eve* and later for a film bearing the same name.[51] Born in 1927, Chris Sizemore (née Costner) may be described as an American housewife of pleasing appearance and with a slight trace of Southern drawl in her speech. As a child she had sometimes suffered sudden bursts of violent and rather unusual behaviour, such as wrecking her cousin's watch or tearing to pieces a dress that her mother had made for her, and after each such occasion justified herself by saying that it had been done by "the other". During adolescence she suffered from violent headaches, periods of hysterical blindness and amnesia, and completely incomprehensible fits of utterly wicked behaviour, during which – to give just an example or two – she might drown a cat or even push her younger sister into an open fire. At twenty years of age she married a man to whom her psychiatrists refer under the pseudonym of Ralph White (so that we, too, shall henceforth call her Mrs. White) and bore him a baby daughter.

One day Dr. Thigpen received a strange and unsigned letter, although both the handwriting and the contents clearly attributed it to Chris. At a certain point the text in Chris' own hand came to an abrupt end and it seemed as if it had been continued by another person with a series of rather crude expressions that were wholly out of line with the earlier part of the letter and also scrawled in a different and undoubtedly less mature hand. When Mrs. Chris White went to see the psychiatrist some time later, he made some reference to this letter and, surprisingly enough, heard her deny that she had ever sent it, even though she remembered that she had been writing it. At this point and before the doctor's very eyes, the timid and hesitant Mrs. White seemed suddenly to become transformed into another person. The physical features of the woman were still the same, but her attitude and expression underwent a complete change, as also did her manner of speaking and even her voice. Crossing her legs, the "newcomer" began to speak with the impudent self-assurance of an insolent young hussy bent on sexual provocation. Almost instinctively, Dr. Thigpen immediately asked her: "Who are you?" "I'm Chris Costner," came the reply. And to the question "Why are you using that name instead of Chris White?" the new personality replied with a decided "Because Chris White is *her*, not me." The two personalities could hardly seem more different from each other. It soon appeared that the letter had been finished and mailed by Chris Costner without Chris White knowing anything about it at all.

Similarly, on an earlier occasion, it had been Chris Costner who had bought some extravagant dresses, with a hemline well above the knee, that had caused a great deal of embarrassment to Chris White when she found them in her wardrobe without being able to give any kind of explanation to her indignant husband. Unlike Mrs. White, Chris Costner smoked cigarettes and expressed herself in less restrained language that, quite often and willingly, became outrightly vulgar. It is particularly interesting to note at this point that electroencephalograms of the subject made respectively when one or the other of these personalities prevailed, were completely different from each other and seemed to relate to two entirely different persons.

"Chris White" and "Chris Costner" were soon joined by yet another personality that emerged under the name of "Jane Doe". This third personality had the connotations of a type intermediate between the other two: cold and sure of herself, with the voice and the manner of speech of a cultured and well balanced person, without the striking defects of "Chris Costner" and yet more mature, alive and interesting than "Chris White". Thigpen at first tried to promote the integration of these two personalities in the newly discovered personality of "Jane", since this seemed to him to be the best of the three. But he soon realized that he was making a great mistake, because the personality of "Jane", which he had nurtured with much love and devotion, also revealed itself to be the most superficial of these three personalities.

"Jane" rapidly filled in certain initial cultural gaps and ended up by constructing for herself a fictitious past that was quite different from that of "Chris White". To this end she modelled her personality, her individual history and even her voice on those of Elen, one of Chris White's cousins. Elen had studied at Furman University and Jane, basing herself on all the things that Elen had related about her life there, began to construct her own personal "recollections": she, too, had studied there and remembered everything about it, from the layout of the buildings right through to campus usages, right down to the names of "her" professors, what they looked like, and not even forgetting their facial tics. She became so convinced of all this that at a certain point she wrote to Furman University to obtain a certificate of the courses she had attended there and remained greatly shocked when some time later she received a curt reply to the effect that, according to University records, no Jane Doe had ever studied there. As already mentioned, "Jane" was the most superficial and ephemeral of the three personalities and she soon "died", ceding her place to a whole series of other minor personalities.

Altogether, the psychiatrists were able to identify as many as thirteen distinct personalities that emerged during the adolescence and adult life of Chris Sizemore, and to this one has to add nine other alternating personalities associated with childhood. These latter nine were all of the same age as the generating personality, while some of the thirteen adolescent and adult personalities claimed different ages, younger or older as the case may be, and in each case the manner of speaking and writing, as also the general behaviour pattern, were entirely in keeping with the presumed age.

Wilson also reports various other cases of alternating personalities, expressly mentioning the researches and the therapeutic practices of Morton Prince (in the classic case of Clara Fowler, which dates back to 1898), Cornelia Wilbur, and George Harding.

What is particularly significant is Wilson's general conclusion in connection with the phenomenon of alternating personalities: "The personalities do not have an extraterrestrial origin, but can be traced back to the characteristics of real-life persons who have formed a strong impression upon the sufferer." Taking something from each, the patient "has then personalized them and unconsciously developed them into a character of his own . . . In short, each personality is nothing more than a satellite, a superficial fragment split off from the parent individual as a result of extreme stress – yet from our point of view the equally important aspect is that each is extraordinarily convincing."(52)

I think that some people may raise a small objection as regards the first few words of Wilson's conclusion, when he says that the personalities disassociated from the fundamental and ordinary personality of an individual "do not have an extraterrestrial origin", etc. Not everybody will agree with this, because there are many phenomena of this kind that seem to suggest that the personality of a "live" person may be temporarily possessed by the personality of a deceased. Extensive literature exists as regards this matter and the claim that many of these phenomena are really cases of temporary "possession" cannot be confuted without a thorough study. This said, however, it seems to me that Wilson's conclusion, taken as a whole, is perfectly correct.

Wilson holds that all the presumed previous incarnations brought out by hypnotic regression can be explained by means of the same mechanism that, operating at the level of the unconscious, generates the alternating personalities we have just discussed. This mechanism can be described as being a kind of self-hypnosis. Given a subject suffering from this particular pathological situation, one may say that every time one of these personalities comes to the fore in him, he "is in a sense locked in a form of self-hypnosis".(53) Indeed, the personalities of presumed previous lives and the alternating personalities of multiple-personality patients reveal something more than considerable behavioural affinities. Each personality, be it of the one type or the other, tends to have a highly characteristic expression of its own and altogether different from the others. Not only each "incarnation", but often also each alternating personality of one and the same subject, has a different image even of its own body. The accent changes, often even the voice. The style of writing changes, and so does the hand itself.

The coherence with itself and difference from all the others that characterizes each of these personalities, "reincarnated" or alternating as it may be, is sometimes pushed to the point where, in one and the same individual, one of the personalities can speak a language that the other does not understand at all. Clara Fowler, for example, spoke French, a language that was completely unknown to her alternating subpersonality that put itself forward under the name of "Sally Beauchamp".[54]

Here is another example of the same type. Don, a young Californian of Japanese origin, spoke nothing but English, even in his own family, and knew but a few words of the language spoken by his forebears. But when he was hypnotized by Professor Erika Fromm and regressed to the age of three years, he suddenly started speaking fluent Japanese and kept it up for more than a quarter of an hour. He was born just before the Second World War and at that age he found himself in a camp where American citizens of Japanese origin had been interned as a precautionary measure and there, of course, Japanese was widely spoken.[55]

Now, irrespective of whether we are speaking of alternating personalities, age regressions or regressions to presumed previous lives, one cannot but stress once more the hypnotic component that is common to them all. It is a well known fact that hypnotic suggestion, and this applies equally to hypnotic self-suggestion, can cause a subject to live a given experience with extreme and even dramatic intensity. In certain cases, the subject may not only become prey to particularly intense feelings, but may even suffer tremendous physical pain without any external stimuli acting on his bodily senses. In a state of hypnotic or self-hypnotic trance, indeed, the subject, as a result of nothing other than suggestion or self-suggestion, may come to bear, in addition to the atrocious pain he feels, also the "stigmata" of his sufferings impressed on his own body.

At the age of almost fifteen, for example, Chris Sizemore quite spontaneously and unexpectedly relived an accident to which she fell victim when she was only three years old, at which time she had come too close to a gas-fired water-heater and her clothes caught fire. Suddenly, therefore, the fifteen-year-old girl began to scream with a child's voice: "Mummy, I'm burning! Mummy, I'm burning!" and really sounded like a three-year-old. The members of her family came running and, on reaching her, noted that the scars that the burns had left on the girl's right arm and shoulder seemed to have come to life and were inflamed as if she had just been scalded again, so much so that when a wet towel was applied to them, it actually began to give off steam.[56]

Wilson draws a parallel between cases of this kind and what – in the strict sense of the term – is normally known as the phenomenon of stigmatization. In this connection he points out that the wounds of the stigmatised, even though they have as their underlying model something that is truly unique, namely the wounds inflicted on Jesus Christ, in actual fact invariably correspond to an altogether personal image of Christ's passion that the individual concerned carries with him: the wounds thus vary both in form and in specific location, and on more detailed investigation are found to coincide, for example, with the wounds depicted on a crucifix in front of which the person used to pray.[57]

In 1928, Dr. Alfred Lechler began to study a subject known as Elisabeth K., born of a peasant family in the southern part of Germany in 1902. The young woman suffered from headaches, vomiting, intestinal disorders, paralyses, fainting fits, insomnia, and so on, and various therapies attempted by Dr. Lechler, electroshock included, produced no result at all. Lechler fully realised that the cause of many of the disorders was of a psychic nature, and quite often the girl showed the symptoms of illnesses that she had merely heard about.

One day in 1932 Elisabeth attended a religious meeting, where slides were used to illustrate the sufferings of the Lord Jesus Christ during his passion and crucifixion. The next time Dr. Lechner saw her she complained about great pain in her hands and feet and when the psychiatrist examined her, he noted all the signs of incipient stigmatization. He therefore decided to use direct hypnotic suggestion on his patient, though not in order to make these wounds disappear, but rather to accentuate them to the greatest possible extent and, subsequently, getting Elisabeth to understand that the origin of the stigmata, as also of other disturbances and illnesses that left their marks on her physique, were solely and exclusively the result of suggestion or self-suggestion.

Subsequent experiments carried out by Dr. Lechner on his patient showed that, irrespective of whether she was in hypnotic trance or in a state of normal consciousness, he could always produce on her body any form of stigmatization he desired, just as he could subsequently make it disappear; similarly, he could get her to participate in a particularly dramatic manner in the various events of Christ's passion, occasions on which she invariably expressed herself as if she formed part of the crowd actually witnessing these events.[58]

If we leave aside all consideration of whether hypnotic regression can or cannot leave physical effects on the subject and, likewise, ignore the problem of the degree and level of such physical involvement, the essential problem that we have to face up to can be defined as follows: is the subject here reliving something that effectively has already been lived by another personality in some earlier period, or is he merely reprocessing experiences made during his present existence on the basis of suggestions he has received from the hypnotist?

We have already noted some of the difficulties one encounters when, quite legitimately, one endeavours to establish a link between the subject's regressive experiences and experiences that he may have made in the course of his present life, because many of these experiences can be easily forgotten, especially in cases where the experiences concerned have not been focused by the subject's attention and have therefore remained – as it were – at the margins of his field of consciousness or even in the background altogether. We have also seen that certain variants of regressive techniques are capable of bringing to light the real genesis of many experiences that the subject at first referred to a previous existence evoked under hypnosis, variants that should therefore always be applied and attempted in such cases. If the regressive technique succeeds and the results can then be confuted by other probant elements, of whatever nature they may be, I would say that the reduction of a seemingly reincarnative experience to an experience of the subject's actual existence can be considered sufficiently convalidated.

Just to take another step forward, I also think that we can undoubtedly exclude all reincarnative interpretations of experiences that are clearly in contrast with history and can clearly be attributed to historical fiction, novels served up in historical fancy dress, pseudohistorical films, television serials and similar products, where truly "all resemblance to real persons or facts that have really happened is purely coincidental", as one so often reads on the title page.

What is more difficult to define, on the other hand, is the suggestive impact that the hypnotist himself, albeit quite unconsciously, can exert on the subject. Here it may be helpful to begin by looking at the cases where this influence is particularly obvious. A journalist publishes two articles on the past-life regressions of Edith Fiore, who immediately becomes "besieged with calls from many people wanting to experience their past lives"; Frederick Lenz, likewise, continues to receive "letters and phone calls from other people who want to share their past life remembrances" with him every time he goes on the air with television or radio shows.[59]

In cases of this kind, therefore, the point would seem to be clearly established, but rather greater difficulties may be encountered when one tries to understand the cases of less forthcoming subjects who, if not altogether sceptical, have an attitude of the type: "I shall believe in your experiments only if you succeed in doing it with me," as one proband is reported to have said to Dethlefsen.[60] If one bears in mind, as Helen Wambach points out, that the beliefs professed by many subjects at the conscious level are very different from the answers they give under hypnosis[61] an aspect that is in any case quite widely known, one is bound to conclude that this suggestive influence is to all intents and purposes always exercised at the unconscious level, and this quite irrespective of whether it is first produced by the hypnotist during the experimental session or whether the subject already comes to him with a conviction that was undoubtedly at first acquired at the conscious level, but by that time has been thoroughly assimilated also by the unconscious.

Dethlefsen is anxious to tell us that he experiments "with anybody, irrespective of whether he believes or does not believe in these experiments, even if he thinks right from the start that it is nothing but a stupid game", and says that he "always obtains the same results".[62] He adds that, at least as far as certain experiments are concerned, he avoids talking about their ultimate purpose, just as he refrains from talking about reincarnation and the like, because he does not want to create any expectations along these lines in the subject; the choice of the subjects and the control of the sessions themselves are left to outside witnesses, once again in order to avoid any suspicion of undue influence.[63]

But the real point here is that the suggestion and influence can be exercised within the limits of the actual session. Dethlefsen induces his subject to go back in time to when he was twenty years old, then ten, five, one, and eventually to the moment of birth, to the prenatal period when he was taking shape in his mother's womb, to the moment of conception. And here, verbatim, is his final suggestion: "And now go back even further until there emerges a new situation. Stop there and start talking about it."(64) Could anybody possibly say that here we do not have a clear hypnotic suggestion to convey to the subject the idea that he must remember experiences of human life that occurred before he was born and, what is more, even before he was conceived?

The same author tells us that, in addition to this comparatively direct method, he also uses another (a less direct and explicit method, as we might say) that begins by considering a particular emotion (some incomprehensible fear of certain things, for example) and then goes back in time in order to uncover the genesis of that emotion. This method seems to be far less successful in tracing previous incarnations, while – as Dethlefsen tells us – "with the first method one almost invariably arrives at a previous life . . .".(65) With that kind of technique, indeed, I should be surprised only if this were not the case.

At this point let us recall the suggestions that Morey Bernstein makes to his subjects which I shall now repeat verbatim, though shorn of the repetitions, so useful in inducing hypnosis. During the first session, after having regressed her to the beginnings of her present existence, Bernstein turns to "Ruth Simmons" (Virginia Tighe) with the following words: "I want you to keep on going back and back in your mind. And, surprising as it may seem, you will find that there are other scenes in your memory. There are other scenes from faraway lands and distant places in your memory . . . Your mind will be going back . . . until, oddly enough, you find yourself in some other scene, in some other place, in some other time . . ."(66) The suggestions imparted during the second session seem even more explicit: "You will find a scene in which you were included, perhaps in some other lifetime, some other age, some other time, some other place."(67) What more can one ask? In fact, Ruth not only regresses to a previous existence, but sets in a distant country, Ireland, to which she is affectively bound by many tales heard and read as a child, reminiscences that, though largely buried in the unconscious, are very closely bound up with the more pleasant reminiscences of the warmth of the family environment.

Let us now see the words used by Helen Wambach, who sometimes hypnotizes also several subjects at one and the same time and at a certain point addresses them as follows: "I want you to go now to the time just before you were born into your current lifetime. Are you choosing to be born?"[68] Subsequently, still in the form of questions, the hypnotist suggests other ideas to her subjects: "Does anyone help you choose? If anyone helps you choose, what is your relationship to the counselor?"[69]. And then again: "How do you feel about the prospect of living this coming lifetime?" Or: "Are you choosing the last half of the twentieth century to experience physical life for a reason? What is that reason?" "Have you chosen your sex for this coming lifetime? If you have, why have you chosen to focus as a man or a woman in this lifetime?" Last question:"What is your purpose for coming into this, your current lifetime?"[70]

Helen Wambach wonders whether she herself may have influenced the answers to some extent. She notes that the majority of her subjects showed a certain reluctance to become reincarnated, while she herself, according to her own reminiscences, was happy and indeed anxious to be reborn. This enthusiasm of hers, certainly, does not seem to have communicated itself very successfully to the other subjects, who do not seem to have read it very clearly in the thoughts of the person who was hypnotizing them and do not seem to have conformed to it as if it were a hypnotic command in the true sense of the term.

Helen Wambach makes use of statistical methods, not least to demonstrate that any presumed influence she, as hypnotist, may have exercised over her subjects was effectively negligible. The facts show, however, that among her 150 mid-West subjects and 600 subjects on the West Coast the number of these who said that they chose to be born amounted to, respectively, 62 and 64 per cent (as compared with 29 and 23 percent who gave clearly negative answers). But this, surely, shows only that the suggestive influence of the hypnotist did not prove to be completely compulsive and cannot by any means be taken as proof that there was no suggestion at all. Rather, one is left with the impression that there was clear suggestion, though it acted only in a relative and partial manner according to the particular subject involved, depending not only on the suggestionability of each individual, but also on his (or her) type and degree of inner maturity.

A truly considerable percentage of Helen Wambach's subjects are said to have dedicated some care and attention to the choice of their present incarnation, seeking counsel, opting for their present sex, etc., and in this they differ markedly from Dethlefsen's subjects, who state that they reincarnated without exercising any options and in a wholly spontaneous, unconsidered manner, automatically, as one is tempted to say. "Just imagine a giant vacuum cleaner that sucks you up, or something like that", one of the German hypnotherapist's subjects actually told him.[71]

A peculiar feature that one notes among Edith Fiore's subjects is the frequency (incomparably greater than in the case of any other similar set) with which, following reincarnation, they find themselves in situations where their close relatives include people with whom they were already closely related (though often in different ways) in previous lives. Let me give you an example of the technique used to obtain these recognitions. Addressing the subject known as "Elizabeth" under hypnosis and speaking of her presumed brother in a previous life (a rather sanguinary character, who had killed and dismembered his wife and three children), Edith Fiore says: "Now, Elizabeth, I want to ask you, is your brother (in the former life) anyone you know in this lifetime?" No answer. The hypnotist therefore resorts to her usual technique of counting up to three: "Who is your brother? What comes to mind at the count of three? One . . . Two . . . Three . . . and what comes to mind?" "My father." "And who is your sister-in law? At the count of three. One . . . Two . . . Three." "My mother." "And the [three] children. Do you know them in this lifetime?" "They are mine." And her children, of course, are likewise three in number, just as in the former "lifetime".[72]

Another feature that keeps recurring among Dr. Fiore's subjects is constituted by the fact that they are often induced to discover that close relatives of theirs did some evil (and sometimes even unmentionable) things to them in previous lives, thus creating traumas and disturbances or other pathological situations in their present lifetime. Even in cases where this realisation leads to a successful (psychoanalytical) therapy, one cannot but wonder whether it would not have been better for the patient to continue living with his obesity, his vertigo, his frustrations or his sexual impotence rather than freeing himself of these disturbances at the price of learning – or getting into his head, one may perhaps be forgiven for expressing the doubt – such horrifying things about the people closest to him.

Enough, no more! It does, however, seem to me that there are various ways in which the hypnotist can exert a suggestive influence on his subject. Indeed, he need not always or necessarily do this by indicating a solution, supplying a possible answer as it were, but can do it just as effectively by asking a question, especially when that question is in itself . . . suggestive, that is to say, when the question is by its very nature full of suggestive force, not least on account of the images that can readily be associated with it or the fascination it can exert on many people; this is particularly true as regards the subconscious, which is well known to constitute the most immature part of the psyche, its most infantile component and the one that most readily allows itself to be enchanted by the glitter and sparkle of certain toys.

While still considering the problem of suggestion, we must now try to give an explanation – or at least an outline of such an explanation – of a problem raised by Dethlefsen when he tells us that he never succeeded in getting anachronistic answers from his subjects during the course of their regressions into past centuries, not even on asking intentional trap questions involving television sets, telephones, motor cars, or tetrapak milk containers: the subject always found such questions strange, failed to understand, and sometimes became annoyed by them. Dethlefsen therefore feels justified in concluding that suggestion has no influence at all on what the subject is going to say. He forgets, however, that the fundamental suggestion is the one that the hypnotist has given from the very beginning, and with full conviction, when he told the subject quite clearly that he could and must regress to a previous incarnation, obviously situated in an earlier epoch, and possibly also to earlier incarnations lying even further back in time. At this point the subject obeys him by regressing to, let us say, the nineteenth century, then the eighteenth, and so on. In so regressing, moreover, his behaviour remains perfectly coherent with the situation. In other words, his regression behaviour is just as coherent as, to give a simple example, that of a Korean orphan who, having forgotten his mother tongue following adoption by a Swedish couple, goes back to speaking Korean as a result of age regression: a moment ago the subject spoke only Swedish, but now – duly regressed under hypnosis – he speaks fluent Korean without any trace of Swedish; rather, on being questioned in Swedish, he doesn't understand a word of it. Each of the two languages, as it were, is contained in a different compartment of his memory. Much the same thing applies as regards the organization of the subject's other cultural notions.

It is quite possible for a subject whose knowledge of France is limited to associating Paris with the Seine and Notre Dame and recalling the overwhelming German victories of 1870 to imagine that the Sun King or an otherwise unspecified King Louis must have sat on the French throne towards the end of the nineteenth century, but surely nobody is so out of step as to be unaware that television and personal computers did not exist at that time. And that is why such subjects, on being questioned in regression, reply that they know nothing about them. Also, taking into account the insistence with which the hypnotist asks these questions and lays these snares, there remains the fact that they are formulated as catch questions and are asked without any real conviction of corresponding to the situation "lived" by the subject; rather, they are often asked with the secret hope that he will pass the test with flying colours, avoid the snare, and thus demonstrate that he cannot be influenced by suggestions.

Another problem arises in this connection, namely to establish whether or not the hypnotist could influence the subject by means of telepathy. Considering this particular aspect, Dethlefsen objects that "one is normally more than content if one succeeds in transmitting some simple images or geometric figures by telepathy," and then adds: "I feel very proud when people think me capable of transmitting entire novels to my patients in this manner." He also says that he himself "expected particular answers, but . . . the effective answers were completely different."[73]

Just as in the case of verbal suggestion, however, it would surely be inappropriate to apply an all-or-nothing criterion to telepathic suggestion: in general principle, at least, the very fact that telepathic communication is so imperfect (and also extremely partial in nature) would make it quite plausible for the subject to react in a partially positive and partially negative manner. The fundamental reaction of Dethlefsen's subjects is substantially in line with his basic thesis, with his fundamental expectations: on this score, surely, he has little or no grounds for complaint.

When all is said and done, therefore, we can surely concur with the conclusion that Simeon Edmunds draws at the end of a chapter dedicated to hypnotic regression in a book about the psychic powers of hypnosis: "All this does not mean that reincarnation *cannot* be a fact . . . But I do believe – and this is what I have tried to show – that reincarnation has not been demonstrated by hypnotic age regression or by any other process connected with hypnotism."[74]

Taken as a whole, indeed, everything we have so far noted about phenomena of the reincarnation type obtained in a state of hypnosis cannot but appear highly suspect. Considered more closely, *the phenomena provoked by means of hypnosis no longer suggest reincarnation,* as they seem to do at first sight, *but rather* – and I would even say clearly so – *suggest the formation of secondary personalities with characters and biographies that are wholly in line with the subject's unconscious psyche* (which, at least in certain cases, can be creative to a very high degree) and, likewise, *in keeping with the suggestions imparted by the hypnotist,* albeit – as often seems to be the case – without being aware thereof (especially when the hypnotist does not realize just how completely the subject is in his hands in this situation, how weak and extremely vulnerable he is to every suggestive influence exerted on him, even if this is no more than implicit).

Even if we were to grant that there are some phenomena in hypnotic regression, or even a goodly number of such phenomena, that could be genuinely defined as suggesting reincarnation, it is precisely the method used to ask the questions that arouses such strong suspicion. Suggesting, at least for the moment, that this category of phenomena should be left out of consideration and kept in cold storage until such time as the experimenters working in this field will themselves introduce the changes in their methods necessary to dispel the doubts that at present attach to them, doubts that are not by any means "just marginal".

CHAPTER III

Spontaneous Phenomena

AT this point we can pass on to considering spontaneous reincarnation phenomena. The most accurate and systematic research for investigating these phenomena has undoubtedly been employed by Ian Stevenson, an American psychiatrist and professor at the University of Virginia, Charlottesville. Unlike other authors who limit themselves to reporting cases, Stevenson personally visits the places concerned, so that with the help of assistants he can question all the possible witnesses.

Stevenson concentrates his attention on cases of children, that is to say, children who suddenly have the experience of being another person, of having the memories of that person; these memories are often found to consist of very lively and detailed reminiscences that can be objectively verified and leave their mark in the mentality of the subject, in his tendencies, tastes and habits, in his manner of expressing himself.

Since the other person is always deceased, the infantile mentality of the subject readily lends itself to the persuasion of being the reincarnation of that other person, a view that is generally in harmony with that constitutes a commonly accepted belief in the given environment. What normally happens is that, following some very upsetting interior experiences, the subject at first has the impression of being that other person rather than himself, and only at a later stage, little by little, succeeds in becoming reconciled with his effective present personality. It is at this point that the familiar idea of reincarnation comes to his aid, helping him to reconcile the fact of feeling himself to be his present self with the fact that at the same time he also feels himself to be that other person: the other assumes the connotation of a previous incarnation of the same ego. Being temporally situated in the past, the other gradually moves out of focus and becomes more remote, while the subject keeps strengthening his sense of identity, concentrating it increasingly in his present personality.

Within the limits of the possible, Stevenson also tries to follow the personal histories of each subject in the years following the period when the phenomenon seemed to explode in him; he thus follows the life of these subjects also in later years, when the small child becomes a boy, an adolescent, and so on, years when they sometimes reabsorb the personality of the "other" to such a point as seemingly to cover it with a blanket of oblivion.

In 1966 Stevenson published his book *Twenty Cases Suggestive of Reincarnation*,[75] which, appreciating the fact that it was subsequently followed by four other volumes of *Cases of the Reincarnation Type*,[76] remains his fundamental work, a real milestone among the literature which many different scholars have written about these phenomena. The twenty cases studied in detail by Stevenson and his collaborators were selected from about two hundred cases that were personally investigated, and they therefore constitute a sufficiently valid point of reference. The reported cases occurred in India and Sri Lanka, in Brazil, in South-East Alaska (among the Tlingit Indians), and in the Lebanon. These countries do not by any means exhaust the areas in which Stevenson has come across interesting cases, among which mention should be made of Thailand and Burma, South-East Turkey, and Syria. The book is undoubtedly sufficiently representative to merit privileged attention.

Before analyzing Stevenson's cases and drawing conclusions from them, however, I should like to mention a book written by Dr. Karl E. Muller, a Swiss collaborator of Prof. Stevenson. This book, which is entitled *Reincarnation Based on Facts*[77] and is rather more summary in its approach, collects a large number of cases from other sources, briefly restating them and classifying them under various headings. The book thus documents many different types of phenomena and seems to me to represent the most undated and variegated treatise today available about this rather complex topic (even though the critical aspects of the book can hardly be considered adequate). Following an introduction about the historical development of the idea of reincarnation and its geographic diffusion, Muller defines his methodology and then reviews first spontaneous reminiscences and subsequently also those produced by experimental means (including mesmerism, hypnosis, and drugs). The testimonies of psychics and mystics are also taken into consideration. While Stevenson, bearing in mind the rigorously scientific environment in which he works, limits himself to analyzing the facts without taking up any position, Muller openly professes his belief in reincarnation and, as a convinced spiritualist, takes into consideration even the presumed testimonies of disembodied entities.

Like Stevenson, Muller reports cases of presumed reincarnation in children, though he simply takes them from other sources:[78] he summarizes eighteen such cases in the East and another nine in the Western world. Over and above these, he also relates the cases of three children who give signs of having a certain understanding of the idea of rebirth in general, another three who claim to remember a former existence in the beyond and, lastly, others where the subject's extreme precocity induces one to speak of paranormal perception. In connection with the latter, however, the author himself points out that neither an exceptional talent nor data regarding paranormal knowledge can by themselves constitute proof of reincarnation.[79]

Unlike Stevenson, however, Muller then passes on to considering also cases suggestive of reincarnation that involve adults:[80] although some of these commence in childhood, there are also cases that assume the form of visions and dreams and yet others that involve the experience of *déja vu*, i.e. where the subject has the clear impression of having already seen a place he has never visited and to have already lived that particular moment before. There are cases of recognition of two kinds, namely one-way recognitions, as happens when a reincarnated child recognizes members of his former family or an adult recognizes a reborn friend, and mutual recognitions.[81] Memories can be brought to the fore by living a similar situation[82] or by illness, trauma, fever, stress, and abnormal mental conditions.[83] As in the case of children, adults, too, can show signs of possessing paranormal knowledge.[84]

It is quite rare for there to be a change of sex in these reincarnation memories of adults: men, in particular, seem to be reluctant to recall them.[85] As regards the reincarnation that one presumes must have immediately preceded the present one, Muller speaks of a change of sex as being testified by only sixteen percent of the girls and twenty-three percent of the women involved in these cases.[86]

A chapter of Muller's book is dedicated to experiences of this type by psychics and mystics:[87] there are psychics that seem to remember their former lives or altered states of consciousness (like conscious astral projections) lived in the first person; further, there are psychics who, either in trance or in a state of normal consciousness, see the incarnations of other people.

Muller comments that some people object, pointing out that certain reminiscences do not necessarily speak in favour of reincarnation and could also be explained by heredity. But Muller replies that memory is not transmitted by heredity, indeed, biologists exclude this possibility;[88] further, as Muller goes on to say, heredity cannot be invoked in cases where the apparent rebirth takes place in a completely different family.[89]

The summary character that Muller purposely confers upon his book, which thus stands in striking contrast with the extremely analytical approach of Stevenson's volume, often seems to lead to over-hasty summaries and similarly hurried conclusions based on uncontrolled attestations taken from books written by authors who, frankly speaking, do not always give the impression of being blessed with full mental equilibrium.

Although no single case can be considered as providing proof, it is quite essential to supplement analytical studies with attempts of synthesis, so that the individual cases, linked in a certain manner to the point of constituting a kind of jigsaw puzzle, may obtain some relative confirmation from the fact that some individual examples of very typical phenomena can be found in them. This is exactly what Muller intended to do. And this is also what I shall try to do here, where I must necessarily be extremely succinct, by adducing some examples that seem significant by very virtue of the fact that they are typical and then combining the facts illustrated by these examples in such a way as to make up a kind of large mosaic.

Coming back to Stevenson, we can begin by looking at the case of Prakash, an Indian boy.[90] Of his presumed earlier life Prakash remembered his own name (Nirmal) and the name of his father, his sister and three neighbours, as well as various details regarding the house, the four shops, and a metal safe. After relating that Prakash also recognized various people and places, etc., Stevenson wondered "about the likelihood that a boy of ten might pick up through normal means the kind of information that he showed".[91] Stevenson notes that Prakash had knowledge of the rooms of the house in which he lived in the presumed previous incarnation, and was also familiar with objects and usages; moreover, he recognized the street in which the house stood and showed himself to possess knowledge about the house and some shops as they were when Nirmal was alive, although they had changed by the time Prakash visited Kosi Kalan, the town where he claimed to have lived and situated about six miles from Chatta, home of his actual family.

A particularly striking detail is constituted by the fact that when the boy at long last succeeded in getting himself be taken to Kosi Kalan, he mistook Memo, Nirmal's sister who had not yet been born when he died, with Vimla, an elder sister already alive at that time. All these details, together with the error just mentioned, suggest, as Stevenson puts it, "previously acquired knowledge of past events rather than recently acquired knowledge as the source of Prakash's information about people and places in Kosi Kalan."[92]

Let us now concentrate our attention on some special aspects, even though we shall take them – one by one – from other cases: in this way we shall construct a kind of identikit of a typical reincarnate.

The little boy Jasbir of the Jat family in the village of Rasulpur[93] falls sick with smallpox and is thought to be dead a few hours later, however, he gives some signs of life, beginning to speak after a few days and to express himself clearly after the lapse of some weeks. At this point he declares himself to be the son of Shankar in the village of Vehedi, about twelve miles from Rasulpur. Stevenson underscores the fact that people living in one of these villages rarely have few chances and occasions of going to another, even though it may be only a few miles away. Indeed, in the whole of Rasulpur he found only two men who had actually been to Vehedi. The things Jaspir says about this new personality emerging fits perfectly with the details of the life of a young man of Vehedi, a certain Sobha Ram, who died when 22 years of age. Unlike Jasbir, a member of a low caste, Sobha Ram was a Brahmin. Following this personality change, the subject, who kept saying of himself "I am the son of Shankar of Vehedi", refused to eat the customary food of his family and for a year and a half accepted only foods chosen and prepared according to Brahmin custom. Then, little by little, his intransigence became attenuated and he slowly readapted to eating the food of the Jat family, though he continued to feel as if in exile in their midst. Immediately after his illness, moreover, people noted a change in the child's vocabulary, who began to call things by names customary among the higher classes. There are also many other interesting details associated with this case, but for the sake of brevity I must refrain from mentioning them and I shall necessarily have to do likewise for the other cases to be mentioned here.

In the case of Sukla,[94] an Indian girl, the noteworthy feature is constituted by the fact that – at one and a half years of age – she was surprised handling a cushion or a piece of wood and calling it "Minu". When asked who Minu was, she replied "my daughter". In the course of the next three years she named several people and also the place where they were to be found, eventually persuading her family to take her there. She then guided her accompanying relatives to the house in question, where in the midst of great emotion she recognized her presumed daughter and her presumed husband. To all appearances the things she had been saying about herself referred to a woman who had died eleven years earlier.

Swarnlata,[95] a baby girl three and a half years of age, was travelling with her father and passing through the town of Katni when she unexpectedly asked the driver to turn into a certain side-street that led to "her house". No notice was taken of her request but, on stopping for tea soon afterwards, the little girl suggested that they should all go to her nearby home, where the tea was much better. Subsequently she supplied details about her presumed previous life in Katni as a member of the Pathak family (which she expressly named) and also performed dances and songs that, as far as her parents could tell, she had not had the chance of learning. These and many other details corresponded to the life of Biya, a woman of the Pathak family who had died twenty years earlier. Another noteworthy feature is constituted by the fact that Swarnlata, though behaving like a little girl in her "actual" family, completely changed her manner when she was in the company of the family of her presumed previous life, where she played the part of Biya and behaved like an elder sister with men who appeared to be at least forty years older.

Two men kill a six-year-old boy, Ashokumar, and cut off his head. Six months later, a baby boy is born in a locality a certain distance away and given the name of Ravi Shankar.[96] As soon as he had learnt to speak, the newcomer began to ask for toys that had belonged to Ashokumar and eventually ended up by describing the manner in which the other child had been assassinated as if it had been done to him. The father, afraid of possible reprisals, did not want to hear him talk like that and did everything possible to discourage him, sometimes even to the point of a beating. Little by little, however, the story came out all the same, and with an impressive wealth of detail corroborated by the facts. Ravi Shankar had a birthmark on his neck that bore a striking resemblance to the kind of wound that would be inflicted by a long knife.

One should also underscore the fact that, following a period in which the boy lived the situations of his presumed previous life with great intensity, he tended to forget the previous existence, slowly shedding also the desires and phobias that went with it, and became increasingly well adapted to his effective existence. On the basis of the "twenty cases" studied by Stevenson in the book that bears this name one can say that, if the statements and the behaviour connected with the previous personality commence between the age of one and a half and four and a half years, they will last for a period that ranges from a minimum of two years to a maximum of sixteen. In the cases where this duration was clearly ascertained, it amounted on average to a little more than seven years.[97]

Stevenson also points out that a change of sex between the two personalities was noted comparatively rarely in a total of about six hundred cases that seemed to provide some confirmation of the reincarnation hypothesis and occurred only in about 10% of the cases. Ceylonese girl by the name of Gnanatilleka[98] appeared as the reincarnation of a boy, Tillekeratne, revealed some masculine trends and characteristics, but began to lose them in adolescence and continued to develop in every respect like a normal woman. In Brazil, again, Emilia Lorenz, who had died at the age of nineteen, became "reincarnated" in a posthumous brother named Paul,[99] who at five years of age and without any prior instruction displayed, among others, an extraordinary dexterity in needlework that were closely reminiscent of Emilia's accomplishments. He also refused male clothing and, taken on the whole, female characteristics seemed to predominate in him; though he later tended to lose these, they never disappeared completely.

Stevenson reports seven cases suggestive of reincarnation among the Tlingit Indians in South-East Alaska. In that region belief in reincarnation, probably imported from Buddhist Asia, was a fact long before the arrival of whites of European origin. It is believed that reincarnation occurs essentially within the limits of one and the same family, and a great deal of importance is attached to bodily signs as proof that a certain person who had these characteristics is reincarnated in a given child. It is quite common for persons on the point of death (or who know that they are going to die) to say that they will reincarnate in the same family and that they are going to have certain characteristics or are going to learn or do things that they had not been able to do in their actual existence. Thus, William George expressed the desire of being reborn as the son of his son Reginald, to whom he bequeathed his old gold watch. He also told him that, on being reborn, he would again have two large birthmarks in prominent positions, one on the left shoulder and one on the left forearm. He died at sixty years of age and, seven months later, was seemingly reborn in his grandchild William George, junior, who had the same birthmarks and also other characteristics of the personality of his grandfather, including the same highly personal and quite abnormal manner of walking. When chance made him come across the gold watch, he exclaimed "That's my watch" and continued to call it such on several other occasions. It is clear that heredity can play a considerable part in these things. But the limping gait of William George, senior was the result of an accident and geneticists deem it extremely improbable that acquired characteristics can be inherited (and many even say that it is altogether impossible).

As regards the birthmarks, Stevenson remarks that "genetics can only point to the probability of inheritance of the moles by later generations. It does not contribute to our understanding of why in this case William George, junior, alone out of all the ten children in this family had moles at the sites of his grandfather's moles."[100] These characteristic body marks, which are said to reappear exactly as they were in the reincarnated person, are a recurring feature of these cases among the Tlingit Indians in Alaska.

The last of the twenty cases reported by Stevenson in the book under consideration is set in the Lebanon and, more particularly among the Druses, a people already mentioned. as believing that rebirth occurs immediately after death. The body in expectation has in the meantime developed in the mother's womb. When the "reincarnation" occurs after a certain interval, as in the case about to be described, the Druses say that in reality there was some other life interposed to bridge the gap.

But now let us take a look at the case in question. Before he was two years old, the boy Imad Elawar[101] of the village of Kornayel began to refer to a previous life, sometimes talking to himself, sometimes talking in his sleep, and also by enquiring about certain people whom he mentioned by name. At a certain moment he spoke about a village called Khriby and a family by the name of Bouhamzy, and then kept asking insistently that his parents should take him there. His father discouraged these requests and got the boy to stop them.

Let me say here, that in these twenty cases there is a predominant tendency not to encourage accounts, testimonies and reminiscences of this type; indeed, they are often thought to be portents of misfortune and signs that the child will not live long, this being especially true in the cases of the Tlingits.

Coming back to the boy Imad, however, he continued to mention names of many people of this other family, which he could not have known in a normal way, gave quite a good description of the home of the late Ibrahim Bouhamzy with a lot of detail, and also spoke about a beautiful woman by the name of Jamile, who had been his mistress; furthermore, he gave a lot of detail about an accident and the quarrel to which it had given rise between the bus driver and the man who had been hit. He also recognized many places, etc.

Here are some more small points that are not without interest: Imad did not want to stay with children of his own age, nor did he dress like them, and he always got angry when people reminded him of his age; when he was two years old, he drank maté like an adult and always showed particular interest in this beverage; precocious at school, he very rapidly mastered French, a language well known to Ibrahim Bouhamzy, who had served in the French army; and many of the things he said, the particular expressions he used, showed the conviction and the strength of feeling with which Imad identified himself with his presumed previous incarnation.

It should also be noted that, in line with the aforemenentioned common belief among the Druses, the boy also claimed to remember details about an incarnation between the two mentioned here: he said that in the period between his death as Ibrahim (1949) and his rebirth as Imad (1958) he had lived at Dahr el Ahmar, but could not remember either the name he had at that time or the way in which he had died; in any case, the details he gave were far too vague to justify any attempt to verify them. Among the Druses there are many people with

memories of this kind, which they ascribe to presumed previous lives.
The twenty cases illustrated in Stevenson's book were chosen from
about six hundred that were known to him at the time of the first
edition, but as a result of continued work their number had risen to
more than one thousand three hundred by 1974. What are the author's
general conclusions? One cannot but recognize that he proceeds with
extreme prudence, raising every kind of difficulty in the true fashion of
a devil's advocate. At least as regards the twenty cases reported in the
volume. He concludes as follows: firstly, the idea of *fraud* is rendered
extremely unlikely by the large number of witnesses and the absence of
any apparent motivation; secondly, *cryptomnesia* could only explain
cases that occurred in families who had known the previous
personality; thirdly, *extrasensory perception* can explain some of the
weaker cases, but a great effort has to be made to stretch it to the point
of explaining the richer cases. Having summarized the first three of
Stevenson's conclusions, it may not be out of place to let him state the
other three in his own words.

Fourth point: "Cases showing a specific or idiosyncratic skill which
the subject could not have inherited or acquired in the present life
require some survivalist explanation, either possession or reincarnation.
But we cannot make a choice between these two possibilities from the
study of the skill alone."[102]

Fifth point: "Most other features of the cases also do not permit a
firm decision between hypotheses of possession and reincarnation. The
conformity of the apparent memories of many of the cases to the
psychological 'law' that recognition exceeds recall favours somewhat
the reincarnation over the possession hypothesis."[103]

Sixth and final point: "Cases suggestive of rebirth with congenital
deformities or birthmarks, provided they are well authenticated,
decisively favour reincarnation over possession for the explanation of
these cases, but not necessarily other cases suggestive of rebirth. The
present group does not include any birthmark cases as well
authenticated, or as free of possible avenues of normal communication,
as some of the other cases suggestive of rebirth which do not include
birthmarks. It does, however, contain cases which illustrate the
possibilities which such cases offer for making a clear distinction
between extrasensory perception, possession, and reincarnation".[104]

Stevenson, too, has come under the fire of Wilson's criticism;[105]
but these criticisms, unlike the ones levelled against regressions (which

we saw in the previous chapter) are on the whole rather marginal, and in any case not such as to invalidate the overall results of the painstaking and systematic researches of the American psychiatrist. The fact that two of his collaborators are convinced and ardent reincarnationists cannot by itself constitute sufficient reason for suspecting and invalidating the results, especially when they have been obtained with all the rigour compatible with the given situations.[106]

It is said, not without reason, that comparisons are odious, but the seriousness, accuracy and systematic nature of Stevenson's work are thrown into even sharper relief when his methodology is compared, for example, with the one followed by Hernani Guimarães Andrade, possibly not in general, but at least in the well-known cases of Uncle Ronaldo, said to be reincarnated in his niece Jacira, and the little Roman girl Angelina, thought to have been reborn as Simone in Brazil. Though Andrade enjoys a reputation as a thorough and valid researcher, though the case of Angelina-Simone has been described as "the reincarnation case that has set Brazil agog more than any other" and as "one of the most limpid and convincing",[107] an Italian resident in Rome – and not wholly devoid of critical faculty – cannot but remain literally thunderstruck on reading the account of the case put together by Andrade himself,[108] for it would seem that nobody has even bothered to come to Rome for the purpose of seriously verifying the facts, although this would have provide particularly easy in the case under consideration. If two people – the girl Angelina and a woman called Alfonsa Dinari – had really been killed on the Capitol by the explosion of a kind of toy at the time when Rome was under American occupation, confirmation could have been obtained by doing no more than perusing a collection of newspapers of the period, just as the existence or otherwise of a certain Alfonsa, wife of Gennaro Dinari, could easily have been discovered by visiting the Registry Office of the city of Rome. Likewise, a dictionary could surely have been consulted to decide whether certain words pronounced by Simone were really Italian, but it would seem that even this was only done in a ridiculously approximate manner.

However, Andrade tells us that the fact that the personages in the claimed previous incarnation have not been traced at all does not by any means imply that they never existed;[109] though this may be formally true, it comes but a few lines after a statement to the effect that "the case of Simone is so full of intrinsic evidence that one is practically dispensed from trying to find people who may have known her previous personality or may have lived with her".[110] Indeed! And what are we to say about the other cases, about Jacira as the presumed reincarnation of her uncle Ronaldo? After reading the monograph reporting this case,[111] I can only wonder why a generally esteemed researcher like Andrade should attribute such a great deal of importance to what has all the appearances of a "home-made" reincarnation phenomenon.

Alan Gauld comments in general terms, and I think rightly so, that "the possibility that the child may have picked up information through listening to adult gossip needs however to be thoroughly explored";[112] and this certainly cannot be said to have been done in the Ronaldo-Jacira case.

There is a great deal of information that adult relatives can give to children without realizing it. And what about the influence that they can exercise? Can one ignore the influence that could have been exercised on Simone, and indeed seems to have been exercised, especially by her grandmother? To the extent to which the prudential rule formulated by Gauld is not always effectively observed, one could even invalidate some of the cases suggestive of reincarnation within the same family that Stevenson investigated among the Tlingit Indians in Alaska.

However, even when one takes account of this aspect, as also of the whole series of reasons, for suspicion formulated by Wilson and others and all the possible reductive hypotheses, one still has to admit that Stevenson's impressive case histories contain elements that, without being conclusive, at least strongly suggest that there must be something that becomes "reincarnated" in some way or other. Even Gauld is convinced of this, notwithstanding the fact that he originally set out with a negative attitude vis-à-vis the reincarnationist explanation, for he has gone on record as saying that when a thorough discussion leads to the elimination of alternative explanations, one is still left with the idea of reincarnation and there thus arises the problem that one must either "accept it, or at any rate begin a serious attempt to make sense of it."[113]

When presented with the particularly suggestive phenomena, the problem is that of determining in what sense one can speak of reincarnation: and this inevitably brings us back to the problem formulated at the very beginning of our considerations, namely the questions of "Who or what becomes reincarnated?" But at this point we come back to posing this question on the basis of some elements that are rather more substantial than the ones we were left with at the end of the previous chapter.

CHAPTER IV

Reincarnation and Possession

The overall picture that emerges from an accurate and critical appraisal of the reported phenomena of the reincarnation type is an extremely complex one, so much so that to me it seems simplistic to hold that a given soul having a specific identity of its own, a continuity with itself as it were, becomes incarnated first in a bodily personality A, then in a physical personality B, and so on. Considered with the attention it merits, reincarnation no longer seems as linear as a thread passing through a series of pearls, but rather resembles a highly tangled skein of wool. One somehow has to get hold of an end and try to untangle it.

After a great deal of meditation on the matter and repeatedly turning the available material inside out, I thought that a re-examination of the case of Jasbir, which I have already recounted in broad outline, could well constitute the starting point for a series of considerations that may throw some light on the problem rather than complicating it even further.

Let me note, first of all, that both Stevenson and Muller[114] include the case of Jasbir among the cases in support of reincarnation. I want to stress this, because the case differs from the classical reincarnation pattern: seemingly, indeed the personality of Sobha Ram, following his death in an accident in May 1954 at the age of twenty-two, becomes reincarnated in the body of the boy Jasbir, three and a half years old, at the time when Jasbir is sick and passing through a crisis such as to be given up as dead. Let me recall that Jasbir subsequently recovered his faculties, little by little, and after a few weeks succeeded once again in expressing himself fully and clearly. At this point his personality seemed to have changed: he declares himself to be the son of Shankar of the village of Vehedi, refuses all food not prepared in Brahmin fashion and, what is more, "remembers" – let us call it so – and "recognizes" some forty odd names of people, things, places, etc., all as ascertained during Stevenson's inquiry and reported in the summary table appended to the account of the case. Stevenson uses the term "exchange incarnation" to describe this case and says that he is currently studying another one of the same kind.[115] Let us therefore adopt this term to indicate phenomena of the Jasbir type.

We can throw a little more light on matters by opening Muller's book on the page where he quotes from Jean Rivière's *A l'ombre des monastères thibetains* (In the Shadow of the Tibetan Monasteries) Rivière tells us that he witnessed the ceremonies that took place on the occasion of the death of the Lama Mé Thôn-Tsampo, abbot of the Tibetan monastery of Ky-rong. Astrologers and magicians had found an eight-year-old boy who had been chosen to be the body of the lama for his next incarnation. The boy was brought on a kind of stretcher and put down on the knees of the abbot's embalmed body, both being then covered by a veil. Suddenly a shout was heard and the boy leapt out from under veil, saying: "I am the Lama Mé Thôn-Tsampo . . ." As Rivière notes, a radical change seemed to have come over the boy: although only a few moments earlier his expression had been decidedly a childish one and he had seemed frightened and unable to understand what was happening around him, a new sparkle had come into his eyes and he was speaking with authority and conviction, with doctrine and in prophetic tones. By way of proof, a number of objects were then put in front of him and the boy, without any hesitation at all, picked out four or five of them, saying: "This is my rosary, this is my teacup", etc. From that moment onwards he was the head of the monastery.[116]

In this case Muller feels himself to be fully authorized to speak of an *obsession*. Everything in the boy's new behaviour goes to indicate that henceforth he will not be a simple medium, a body that will enable the late abbot to express himself by possessing it from time to time, but rather a permanent incarnation of the old head of the monastery, a means for ensuring the constant presence of the deceased abbot. *Obsession*, therefore, in a sense that is rather more specific than the generic term *possession*. What, indeed, is an obsession? "In metapsychics," as Ugo Dèttore puts it, "the term is used to describe a particular case of possession or alternating personalities in which the subject seems to be possessed by the personality of a deceased person either permanently or for a more or less long period of time."[117] Muller, though seeing things from his own viewpoint, notes that some obsession cases seem to be connected with reincarnation.[118]

I should like to stress here that in the last resort certain phenomena of the reincarnation type seem to coincide or, at least, to display marked analogies with cases of obsession. The case of Jasbir is particularly significant in this connection. Stevenson includes it among the cases that *suggest reincarnation* and, as we have seen, Muller also considers it as such. On the other hand, one can hardly overlook the strong analogies that seem to exist between "exchange reincarnation" cases of the Jasbir type and cases of obsession or, more precisely, stable possession, for both phenomena, at least in the early stages, seem to be characterized by a kind of personality change.

When one speaks of obsession, one is almost immediately led to think of the phenomena of so-called obsession or possession by the "devil". We can indeed begin by considering these particular phenomena, but only after making it clear that such manifestations attributed to demons do not by any means exhaust the phenomenon of obsession, which is far more variegated and, in many cases, can also express positive intentions.

In taking a look at phenomena of presumed diabolic origin, we can begin by concentrating our attention on a particular case reported by Corrado Balducci in his book *La possessione diabolica* (Diabolic Possession). Before doing so, however, there are three points I should like to clarify.

Firstly, let me say that when Balducci restricts his analyses to phenomena presumed to be of demoniac origin, he prefers the term "possessed by the devil" to the more traditional "obsessed by the devil" because, as he points out, "here we are not concerned with a disturbance (not even one that springs from within the body), but rather with a usurpation of dominion, an occupation, a possession that confers upon the devil the characteristics of a master."[119] But I prefer in this case to speak of *obsession,* because this enables me to conform to the aforementioned terminological distinction explained by Dèttore and to make it clear that I am referring not to *temporary possessions* (like the ones that occur when an extraneous personality seems to take possession of a medium for the duration of a trance and do not extend beyond this time), but rather to *stable possessions* that last, at least, for longish periods of time. Muller, too, speaks of *obsessions* in this particular sense.

There is also a second distinction it will be useful to make: subject to assumption that an invisible personality really does take possession of a second personality incarnated in a physical body, this possession, quite irrespective of whether it be temporary (lasting, for example, no more than the duration of a spiritist séance) or assumes more or less stable connotations (obsession), can in either case occur – as it were – either as a *partial* possession or as a *total* possession. We therefore find ourselves with four different series of phenomena that we propose to denominate as follows, illustrating each case with an appropriate example:

1) *Partial temporary possession,* as happens in cases where a mediumistic personality (i.e. a "spirit" or somebody purporting to be such) does no more than expressing itself through the medium, though the medium remains "awake" and feels that personality as "another" and may even dialogue with it.

2) *Total temporary possession,* as in cases where the mediumistic personality assumes complete control of the medium, who sinks into a profound trance and loses consciousness, so much so that he cannot remember anything at all upon reawakening.

3) *Partial stable possession,* as in cases where the invisible personality that has become installed in a "living" person limits itself to an action of disturbing or, going to the other extreme, helping that person, or (as happens in other cases) giving rise to artistic or literary creation through the person acting as medium, who always feels the "invading" personality as "another".

4) *Total stable possession,* which occurs in cases where the possessing subject occupies a person to the point of cancelling that person's consciousness; in this case, once again, nothing is remembered when possession ends.

And here is my third point: it does not by any means follow that in "diabolic" possessions the possessing subjects must always or necessarily be identified as demoniac entities, i.e. as "demons" or "devils" or as "*the* Devil", all of which are entities that we know little or nothing about and therefore represent notions that are perhaps better left out of our considerations, all the more so as they remain more or less alien to them. Indeed, many of the "devils" confess that they were once men living on this earth, a good example of this type being represented by the devil in the case so minutely described by Balducci,[120] a devil that then remains to obsess "Marcella" after nine others have been driven out of her by exorcisms of various kinds. This devil admits to being a deceased person and one may, perhaps not unreasonably, assume that this is equally true for many others. However this may be, one cannot but note that they act and express themselves in a manner that is strikingly similar to what human beings are wont to do, and this no matter what fanciful "nom de guerre" or diabolic grade or title they may use to introduce themselves. Indeed, one cannot even exclude here the coming into play of unconscious personifications of the type associated with "alternating personalities" and similar phenomena.

And now let us turn to Balducci's devils. There are three cases that he describes in great detail in the book. In the case of "Marcella" (personally known to the author and referred to by a pseudonym) one may note that the girl is well aware of being the victim of a possession and desires to break free of it. There are moments when the things she does and says are expressions of herself and at such times she gives proof of the best of intentions; but there are also times when the demoniac personality gains the upper hand, which causes her to change expression and to do and to say things that would never occur to her of her own accord. Here, therefore, we have a case involving some kind of alternation. Something very similar can be said about the "bedevilled woman of Piacenza", the second case described in Balducci's book.[121]

But the third case, the "possessed of Illfurt",[122] is very different, for here we see diabolic personalities gain possession of two Alsatian boys, Theobald and Joseph Burner, respectively nine and seven years of age, maintaining this state of affairs for as much as five years. For the whole of this period the two boys neither behaved nor spoke in their usual manner, but displayed a change of personality altogether analogous to the one that, *mutatis mutandis*, we already had occasion to note in the case of Jasbir: the boys no longer seemed themselves, not even intermittently. They returned to being their normal selves only after they had been liberated by means of adequate exorcisms. As soon as he had been abandoned by the two "demons" that had occupied him, Theobald once again became the cheerful, quiet and rather insignificant boy he had been before; at this point he recalled nothing of what had happened, did not recognize either the exorcists or his parish priest, and was surprised by the strange behaviour of his brother, who was still under the spell of the devils. Let me quote from the same source used by Balducci:[123] after his liberation, Theobald, "having brought some blessed medals from Strasbourg, offered one to Joseph and remained astonished when his brother threw it on the floor and stamped on it, shouting angrily: 'You could have kept it for yourself, I don't need it'. 'Has Joseph gone mad, mummy?' asked Theobald, who could find no other explanation for his brother's strange behaviour, which his mother was not by any means anxious to explain to him."

But even here we seem to be concerned with a personality substitution, something – that always provided that we ignore the demoniacal character of this particular phenomenon – can be likened to "exchange incarnation" cases of the Jasbir type. For the moment I shall dwell on the elements of analogy that seem to be common to cases *suggestive of reincarnation* similar to what happened to Jasbir and cases of total stable possession, deferring the problem of the differences to a later stage (without in any way denying that these differences could be profound and even essential).

I pointed out earlier that the phenomena of obsession (i.e. of stable possession) do not always seem to be manifestly "diabolic". At the opposite extreme, indeed, there is a wide range of obsession phenomena that seem to derive from benevolent intentions, while in between they seem to occur in haphazard fashion as it were and without any clearly defined bias for either good or evil.

The most famous of the cases of stable possession that can be included in this intermediate category is the one known as the "Watseka Wonder".[124] In 1865 there died, at the age of nineteen years, an American girl by the name of Mary Roff, while a year earlier the Vennum family (which subsequently moved to Watseka, the town where the Roffs were living) was blessed with the birth of a baby daughter, Mary Laurancy Vennum. In July 1877 Laurancy, then thirteen years of age, began to have strange fits in the course of which she lost consciousness. This came to the ears of Mr. Roff, who remembered that his own daughter had had similar attacks and counselled the Vennums to have Laurancy examined by Dr. Stevens, a physician of his acquaintance. When Laurancy had some of these crises, she spoke of herself first as an old woman by the name of Katrina Hogan and then as a young girl named Willie Canning. Once, after a particularly violent attack, Dr. Stevens succeeded in calming Laurancy by hypnotizing her. In this state she told him that she had fallen prey to evil spirits, and Dr. Stevens therefore suggested that she should entrust herself to a good spirit. To this the girl – still under hypnotism – replied that the spirit of Mary Roff was standing by, ready to come to her aid. And thus it was, to all appearances at least, that the late Mary Roff came to take possession of the personality of Laurancy Vennum. Muller regards this as a case of obsession,[125] and if we want to allocate it to one of the four distinct categories listed earlier, we can consider it as a case of *total stable possession* that bears some striking resemblances to the case of Jasbir and – leaving devils and demons advisedly aside – also to that of the "possessed of Illfurt".

Let us, however, take a look at the sequel. From that moment onwards Laurancy, though now calm and serene, fully believed that she was Mary Roff. She insisted on wanting to live with the Roffs and when this request was granted, she went to join them in their home in February 1878 and remained there for a little more than three months. She recognized all the persons and things that had in some way been related with the existence of Mary Roff, but no longer recognized the Vennums, considering them as nothing other than friends of the family. Here is an interesting detail: speaking to Dr. Stevens about her previous life, she told him about an injury she had suffered on her arm and wanted to show him the scar; when rolling up her sleeve, however, she suddenly stopped and added: "Oh, this is not the arm; that one is (buried) in the ground." At this point she explained where she had been buried and described her funeral, which she claimed to have seen, listing the people who had been there and what each of them felt at the time.

Early in May, however, Laurancy began every now and again to remember something about her true family and personality. Then, speaking as Mary, she said that she could leave Laurancy's body on May 21, at about eleven in the morning, and this duly happened. Laurancy began to feel herself again and all her former memories returned, but she no longer recognized Dr. Stevens, who had attended her throughout this period. Thereafter the presumed personality of Mary Roff returned only for short periods of trance and Laurancy enjoyed unfailing good health. She eventually got married and when she was about to have a baby, "Mary Roff" caused her to fall into a trance to avoid feeling the birth pains. In marked contrast with that obsession cases are generally thought to be, the Watseka Wonder can therefore be considered as a case of *protective obsession*.

The Watseka Wonder dates to rather long ago, but Stevenson, working in collaboration with Pasricha, studied a very similar case of possession in India in far more recent years. The subject was Uttara

Huddar, a woman who, born in 1941, lives (or lived) in Nagpur, Maharashtra. where she had a teaching assignment at the local university. She was bitten by a snake at the age of twenty-two and from that moment onwards began to have crises of variable duration and characterized by the fact that her normal personality seemed to become replaced by another and markedly different one. This new personality took Uttara's place at least thirty times, the duration of the crises ranging from a day to seven weeks, and called herself Sharada: she seemed to be wholly unaware not only of everything connected with Uttara and her environment, but of all modern life from the industrial revolution onwards. Sharada would seem to have lived as the daughter of a certain Brajanath Chattopadhaya in the years around 1810-30. She spoke excellent Bengali, a language that Uttara said she did not know at all, and proved to have good knowledge of Bansberia, a town to the north of Calcutta, and the surrounding areas, including some out-of-the-way villages and temples, while Uttara again declared that she had never been in Bengal. A family by the name of Chattopadaya still lives in Bansberia today and its family tree includes five men mentioned by Sharada as her relatives (and even in the correct order), but unfortunately does not record any of the women. Although this lacuna makes it impossible to check any of Sharada's female relatives, all other details given by her seem to fit.[126]

In one of his books[127] Ernesto Bozzano reports and analyzes a case that he expressly compares with the Watseka Wonder. He describes both these phenomena as cases of "mediumistic possession of a spontaneous nature and long duration": these possessions are analogous to those that occur in the course of séances, but occur outside such sessions and are of characteristically long duration (days, months, and even years).

Here are the reported facts, however. In the morning of 13 February 1936 the body of a nineteen-year-old bricklayer named Giuseppe Veraldi was found under a bridge that joins the Calabrian town of Catanzaro to its outlying suburb of Siano. Although the nature of the injuries suggested that the young man had been killed and his body then dumped in the ravine in a rather clumsy attempt to camouflage the murder, the judicial authorities eventually concluded that he had committed suicide by jumping off the bridge following an unhappy love affair. Almost three years later, on 5 January 1939, a seventeen-year-old girl named Maria Talarico was passing over the bridge when she suddenly collapsed to the ground in a faint. She was taken home and put to bed, but got very restless and began to call her mother at the top of her voice. Her mother hastened to the bedside, only to hear Maria say in a decidedly male voice: "You are not my mother, but the woman who lives in this house. My mother lives at the Baracche (Huts) and is called Caterina. I am Pepè (Italian diminutive of 'Giuseppe'). Go and tell her to come here right away to see her wretched son." The woman she had described was Veraldi's mother. Not seeing her arrive, Maria – though still in the vestiges of her new personality – then sent another messenger with a written note saying: "Dear Mother, if you want to see me, I am your wretched son." The handwriting was found to be the same as Giuseppe's.

When Mrs. Veraldi eventually arrived, Maria (or, if you will, the late Giuseppe Veraldi incarnated in Maria's body) ran up to her, embraced her with great affection and then, little by little, gave her a detailed account of his tragic end in answer to her anxious questions. Four men, named Totò, Abele, Damiano and Rosario, had invited him to a certain tavern, where they made him drink a large amount of wine to which they had also added some potions; they had then taken him outside, beaten him to death and left his body in the place where it was found next morning. Maria then had many other dramatic encounters, and on all these occasions she always expressed herself as if she were Giuseppe Veraldi come to life again.

In the end Maria's mother, greatly concerned by the state into which her daughter had been reduced, begged "Giuseppe" to abandon the girl's body. The subject, be it Maria or Giuseppe, thereupon went back to the bridge, made its way down to the bottom of the ravine, and stretched out on the ground in the very place where the body had been found three years earlier. Assuming the same position as the cadaver, it remained there as if in a sleep of death. A few minutes later the subject reawoke, but now behaved and spoke once more like Maria. The crisis had lasted for a day and a half, and the girl, seemingly awakening from a long sleep, seemed to have no notion of what had happened. It was later ascertained that she had never been particularly impressed by the news of Giuseppe Veraldi's death and that she had never known him personally.

Another striking detail relating to the period of possession is represented by the fact that at a certain moment the subject, speaking as if it were Giuseppe, declined the offer of food, justifying the refusal by saying that his teeth and jaw were broken (which corresponded to the state in which Veraldi's body had been found under the bridge). The evidence of a non-commissioned officer of the Carabinieri has been summarized as follows: "Sergeant Sità said that he wanted to take a look at the jaw and assured us that he heard a creaking sound coming from the horizontal part of the right jaw. He also wanted to touch the teeth and found them so loose that he had the impression they would come away in his hand."[128]

Dr. Carl A. Wickland's book *Thirty Years among the Dead* is also dedicated to obsession phenomena.[129] The author, a psychiatrist, availed himself of the collaboration of his wife, a medium and sensitive person. In the magnetic "aura" of a subject suffering from psychic disturbances Mrs. Wickland would often perceive the presence of a disincarnate entity. In such cases the patient would subsequently be subjected to currents of static electricity, a treatment that the spirit could not resist for a long time, eventually causing it to change abode by becoming incorporated in the medium. Here are some reported snatches of dialogue between Dr. Wickland and the disincarnate entity in its new abode. When a spirit complained of feeling pain as if pricked by many pins, for example, Dr. Wickland said: "You were influencing a lady and making her cry." Spirit: "What do you mean?" Doctor: "You are a spirit, and were in the aura of that lady. When she had an electrical treatment you felt it and left her. You are using my wife's body now. Look at your hands; do they belong to you?" Spirit: "Oh, look! I have a ring! But that is not mine, and I have not stolen it. (Excitedly) Take it away! I didn't steal that ring." Doctor: "This is not your body, and that is not your ring. It is very likely that you died when your head was hurt. The spirit lives after the body dies."[130] In this way Dr. Wickland succeeded, little by little, in convincing the spirit of his true condition as a dead person, thus causing it to desist from all further obsession, to acquire a more conscious and serene attitude, and to rise to a higher spiritual sphere.

Dr. Wickland dedicates separate chapters to spirits that were unhappily married in life, to spirits that committed some crime, etc. Among these spirits there can be some that are thirsting for vengeance and hope to obtain it by acting through the bodies of individuals sensitive to their influence. Crimes are often committed by people who until a few moments previously were irreproachable in their conduct, behaving in all things as if they were among the most gentle and meek of this earth.

Wickland recalls the case of Frank James, a New York boy of excellent character, who suffered a head injury and lost consciousness; when he regained his senses in hospital, he seemed to have become another person, decidedly quarrelsome and insolent. He soon began to engage in robberies and other criminal activities, so that he had to to be sent first to reformatory on several occasions, then to serve a five-year sentence in Sing Sing, and eventually ended up in a criminal lunatic asylum. He succeeded in escaping from there, but was soon recaptured. In the struggle to avoid capture he was hit on the head again, lost consciousness and had to be taken to hospital. On coming to himself next morning he appeared completely transformed for a second time and had become once more the kind and deferent person he had been before his vicissitudes began; he was mentally sane and no longer had even the slightest impulse to commit the criminal actions for which the law had persecuted him for such a long time.[131]

Obsessive spirits rarely seem to be aware of their true condition. This is the conclusion that Bozzano reaches in his text *Dei fenomeni di ossessione e possessione* (About the Phenomena of Obsession and Possession).[132] He thinks they are deceased people who died while prey to feelings of despair or hate, and sometimes also to perverse instincts or vices. Their frame of mind becomes petrified into a kind of somnambulant monoideism, a state in which the phantasmas of their obsessive ideas become as real and concrete as, for example, dreams seem to a sleeping person or the hypnotist's suggestions to his subject. As a general rule, they believe themselves to be still alive and find themselves prisoners of a kind of nightmare, bent only on sustaining their particular passion. When they succeed in entering the orbit or the magnetic aura of a sensitive person to whom they are bound by some affinity or on whom they can exert some influence, they instigate the person concerned to act in a manner that will enable them to obtain gratification by proxy, by reliving their particular experiences through another person. Although they are prisoners of a form of hallucination, they are nevertheless capable of reasoning. But the form of reasoning here involved is the one that comes to the fore in dreams and in the hypnotic state: it is a "reasoning that even though it leads to the attainment of the desired goal, is yet neither *sensible* nor *judicious*, this in the sense that in it one can certainly find a logic of *execution* but never the logic of *reason*."[133] Obsessive spirits can be more readily and quickly brought out of this kind of dream or nightmare when they are put into contact with the experimenters by means of mediums and hypnotic practices: when such contact is established, they can often be made to "amend their ways".

Irrespective of whether these entities succeed in satisfying the impulses that dominate them by obsessing people living on this earth, it would seem that between this world and that of the deceased there is an intermediate sphere full of entities that have remained bound to our level, the so-called earthbound spirits; these are generally people who died either suddenly or violently, war victims, suicides, people put to death, entities who have remained prey to their passions and unsatisfied desires, spirits moved by hate or cravings for revenge, confused spirits roaming restlessly, victims of a nightmare and often even unaware of having died. It would seem that such afflicted souls can obtain illumination and guidance, comfort and effective help not only from missionary spirits in the world beyond, but also from men and women of good will still living on this earth. For example, a married couple living in Oregon, U.S.A., have dedicated themselves to this task of psychic rescue: the wife, Doris Heather Buckley, interviews the entities with whom she established contact through the mediumship of her husband and tries to help them to come to grips with their problem.(134)

What has been said here about the condition of these earthbound spirits is confirmed not only by traditional spiritist literature, but also by more recent writings about the results of communication with the dead (or entities presumed to be so). A book by Harold Sherman,(135) for example, arrives at the general conclusion that on this earth men behaving in a criminal, homicidal, beastly or lawless manner open the door to being possessed by spirits of a low degree of mental development, this evidently on the basis of the principle that "birds of a feather flock together".

We are also told that "many earthbound spirits, bereft of their physical bodies and obsessed with the desire to return to earth, roam about seeking opportunities to attach themselves to the consciousness of living mortals who may have left themselves open to possession through use of the Ouija board, automatic writing, excessive indulgence in alcohol or drugs, or as the result of nervous breakdowns or sordid misuse of sex."

Basing himself on a long experience of such communication through mediums, Sherman also notes that "there are others whose lives on earth have largely been spent in criminal and unspeakably vicious pursuits, and who are required to suffer the self-punishing experience of dwelling in what has been described as 'dark, dismal areas', where they seem to be fixated on acts of their unsavoury past – a state which might be likened to the Catholic concept of 'Purgatory' or the Christian idea of ' Hell'."[136]

But the satisfaction of passions, vices and low-level attachments does not by any means exhaust the range of motivations that can induce an entity to obsess persons still living in this world. Taken together, these can indeed constitute the gamut of truly low and frequently occurring motivations. But there are also cases in which the motive is more noble: for example, it may be provided by a feeling of love for one's family and the desire to continue living in its midst, as in the case of "Mary Roff" (Watseka Wonder), just as it may consist, to give but one other example, of a desire for artistic expression. A case of this kind was the one of a young man called Thompson, who was permanently afflicted by hallucinatory forms combined with the conviction of being possessed by a deceased painter. He claimed that Gifford, the painter, had induced and inspired him to paint several pictures in his own style, including one of which an absolutely identical sketch was effectively found in Gifford's atelier.

Another interesting case is the one of the writer Frank R. Stockton, who with persecutory tenaciousness took possession of a sensitive lady and would not leave her in peace until she sat down at a desk or table, thus allowing him to write through her hand a series of posthumous novels that were wholly similar to his other work in language, form, construction and inventive fantasy. These and other cases are reported by James Hyslop in the first (and so far only) chapter of a proposed book about obsession phenomena.[137]

Dr. H. N. Banerjee, a parapsychologist who performs his research activities connected with reincarnation phenomena in both India and the United States, reports the more recent case of David Paladin, thought to incarnate the late Wassily Kandinsky, a painter. According to what Banerjee tells us about this subject,[138] David Paladin was born in a Navajo Indian reserve in Arizona, son of an Indian woman and a white missionary. Serving in the American army during the Second World War, he was wounded on the German front and taken to be dead; when he subsequently gave signs of life, he was sent to the

United States, where he remained in a military hospital for two years without regaining consciousness. When he finally did so, in 1946, he said to the nurse who was looking after him: "I am an artist." Although he had never shown any particular talent for painting and had never attended art school, he began to paint abstract pictures as soon as he was eventually released from hospital. His style, which would seem to be greatly appreciated by art critics, bears a striking resemblance to the work of the late Kandinsky. When hypnotized, Paladin spoke English with a Russian accent and was found to be familiar with details of Kandinsky's life, facts that seemingly he could not possibly have known as Paladin.

After having studied the subject, Dr. Banerjee felt justified in concluding that David Paladin "died" in 1944 and that Wassily Kandinsky had become "reincarnated" in him. Let me add, however, that Banerjee makes a clear distinction between reincarnation and possession. Using the Paladin case as example, the essence of this distinction can be explained as follows: If this were a case of possession, Paladin, when painting, would limit himself to letting his hand obey an extraneous force, the spirit of Wassily Kandinsky; the pictures would therefore be painted by the dead artist, with David Paladin reduced to a mere instrument, barely or even wholly unaware of what is happening. But Paladin has perfect mastery of himself while he paints, is fully aware of what he is doing: even though he creates in a state of consciousness that could be said to be altered, in this case one can speak of an alteration that closely resembles that of a poet writing his verses under inspiration. That Paladin does not work as a personality possessed by Kandinsky is also confirmed by the fact that he speaks like Kandinsky only when he is hypnotically regressed to this previous incarnation, be it real or presumed: at the level of his ordinary consciousness he is clearly David Paladin.

It could well be that when he first regained consciousness in 1946, Paladin had lost the sense of his own identity, somewhat on the lines of Jasbir, who – upon regaining his senses after having survived the crisis caused by his illness – no longer recognized himself as Jasbir and was dominated by the idea of being Sobha Ram; but everything leads one to suppose that, just like Jasbir, Paladin eventually recuperated the sense of his own identity, indeed, that he became increasingly sure of it. Banerjee himself notes that Paladin is an artist in continuous evolution. In other words, that in the last resort he leaves behind not only what could be considered a static fidelity to Kandinsky's style, but also his feeling himself to be Kandinsky, i.e. he leaves behind his "being Kandinsky" to become ever more autonomously and creatively himself, Paladin. Ultimately, therefore, he only sees Kandinsky as his own past, as a previous incarnation of himself: he no longer sees Kandinsky as his own personal present, as had been the case at the time of the first impact, at the moment when he had "woken up as Kandinsky". Although accepting the obvious differences, and making all due allowance for the diversity of the two situations, one may say that what happened to Paladin is rather similar to what was later to happen to the little Jasbir.

Jasbir, whose case had been followed by Stevenson (as far as possible) also in later years, never wavered in his conviction that he was a reincarnation of Sobha Ram, and yet he became increasingly reconciled with and adapted to his actual condition, which he accepted for karmic reasons: his declassment, his becoming reincarnated in a family of low condition, was probably due, so he thought, to negative actions he had committed not as Sobha Ram, but possibly in an even earlier incarnation.[139] In any case, he had decided to marry a girl of his present low caste. In the early stages of his vicissitude he had identified himself with Sobha Ram in a far stronger and, I would even say, exclusive manner. He was wont to say of himself: "I am the son of Shankar of Vehedi."[140] Indeed, one could say that he was completely absorbed in the part of the young Brahmin, that all his feelings were involved. But subsequently the boy began to realize quite clearly that Sobha Ram was dead, that he was Jasbir, a member of the Jat family of the village of Rasulpur. The belief in reincarnation, which he obviously could not profess in clear and explicit manner at the time when these phenomena first became manifest within him (he was then only three and a half years of age), helped him in later years to attribute more adequate sense and meaning to his experience: he thus came to consider himself as Sobha Ram, though reincarnated in Jasbir. Indeed, when Stevenson asked him his mailing address, the boy told him to address letters to Jasbir Singh Tyagi, son of Girdhari Lal Jat: in this way, as Stevenson puts it, he accepted the reality of the paternity of his body, but at the same time proclaiming also his membership of the caste to which he had belonged in his previous life.[141]

When faced with phenomena of the kind just reported, it seems to me that one can speak, at least at a certain moment, of a seeming invasion of one personality by another: a phenomenon of possession, in other words. The invading personality can even take the place of the normal personality of the invaded subject, the possessed, relegating it to the depths of the unconscious as it were.

The two personalities can coexist (in which case the second will be "disturbed" by the first, or in some cases also "helped" by it, as happened at Watseka); and they can also alternate, more or less in the manner of the well known psychic phenomenon of alternating personalities, although in this latter case all the psychic material belongs to the same subject and no part of it derives from an invading or extraneous subject.

In the case of obsessed that already feel the benefits of the exorcism, again, the invading personality is to all appearances banished or expelled. Even the personality of Mary Roff eventually announces that it is about to go away. And therefore both in the case of the demon or the "damned soul" that is chased away by means of exorcism and in the case of the good soul of Mary Roff, which goes away of its own accord, we have a complete abandonment of the invaded personality by the invading personality that occupied it for a certain period of time without becoming merged with it, without giving it anything that the invaded personality can take over and assimilate. The two personalities remain distinct.

But something different seems to happen in the case of Jasbir. It is quite true that at first we have to all appearances an invasion of Jasbir by the personality of Sobha Ram or some part of that personality, but the final outcome in this case is a slow and gradual absorption of the personality of Sobha Ram (or some part of it) by the personality of Jasbir. As far as one can judge from the information provided by Banerjee, and it is truly far from complete, something very similar would seem to have happened in the personality of David Paladin.

In other words, one can sometimes observe phenomena of temporary possession or obsession of a personality B by a personality A that do not leave in B an imprint such as to cause a permanent personality modification. In cases of this kind A eventually goes away and leaves B more or less as it was before its arrival. In cases where A really has an effect on the personality of B, on the other hand, it leaves something of itself in B that eventually merges with the erstwhile personality. And it is only in this case, so it seems to me, that one can properly speak of *incarnation*, for it is only in these cases that personality A comes to permeate personality B, communicates itself to it, becomes incarnate in the body of B.

In this second case, i.e. where the two personalities assimilate each other as it were and A becomes englobed in B, one can readily understand that the memories of A may eventually be taken over by B as its own. In this sense, therefore, one can understand quite readily that even in cases where A has lived before B, the personal memories of A can be taken over by B as his own personal memories, not least by virtue of the particular rationalization process that makes these memories coexist with those of B's actual existence by considering them to derive from the existence of the same individual in a previous life.

Another problem arises at this point. As we have already seen to some extent, the invasion of a personality by another – or, at least, a limited invasion by a fragment of this latter – can occur at any time. In the course of its life, therefore, personality B could suffer invasion not only by personality A, but also by A', A", etc. Why, then, does it remember only "having been A?" I think that this happens because other memories are emarginated and excluded under the influence of the mentality of the subject under consideration, who has his own convictions and beliefs and these, in turn, may derive from mentalities and beliefs that are common in the formative environment of the subject.

The fact that reincarnation is generally conceived as a succession of individual lives (each clearly delimited, rather like pearls kept in line by the string on which they are threaded) can induce one to reject the idea of lives that merge or flow into each other, somewhat in the manner of the tributary of a river. A mentality formed under the influence of the more *linear* idea of reincarnation will therefore tend to reject the very different idea that some part of A can become reincarnated in B even years after B has been born, just as this could happen a certain time before A actually dies. This refusal of the idea – or at least difficulty in accepting it – may well take place at an instinctive and unconscious level long before it emerges onto the level of clearly motivated and rational awareness.

Putting this more clearly, we can say that when the subject focuses his attention on his presumed previous lives, when he questions himself about them or tries to put himself in condition to draw upon his memories of them, he *expects* to relive a series of existences in such linear succession. The general expectation is that such existences can be separated by an interval, but among the Druses of the Lebanon, for example, reincarnation is expected to take place at the very moment of death. Elsewhere again, the Tlingit Indians in South-East Alaska being a case in point, the subject expects reincarnation to occur within his own family; if, therefore, a Tlingit Indian has the presumed experience of reliving the series of his previous incarnations, he will quite naturally expect to relive a number of existences in which he was incarnated in, one after the other, his own ancestors. Since the dominant mentality can condition the very nature of the reincarnation phenomena, it is not difficult to realize that it can even more readily condition the series of "memories", be they real or presumed.

It should be noted that most of the phenomena suggestive of reincarnation, as well as most presumed memories of former lives, seem to occur in countries or among ethnic groups where reincarnation constitutes a generally held belief. The present reincarnation boom in our Western world, moreover, could quite easily favour the coming into being in our own midst of phenomena of the reincarnation type on a scale that was quite unknown in the past and, indeed, could hardly have been attained during the long centuries when the West was dominated by Christianity, which considered reincarnation doctrines to be out of bounds.

It should also be noted that, at least as a general rule, reincarnation phenomena and memories seem to conform to the general pattern which a given environment believes reincarnation to be governed. Likewise, one should note the relative scarcity of such phenomena in environments where the idea of reincarnation is not accepted. In Catholic environments, for example, the idea of reincarnation is rejected, but there is a longstanding tradition and widespread belief that people can be possessed by the devil; it is therefore very probable that Catholic environments tend to interpret as possession and obsession phenomena many forms of behaviour that in reincarnation environments would be interpreted as reincarnation phenomena.

One may add that, at least in a certain range of boundary-line cases, the particular beliefs and convictions current in the subject's environment could well induce him to consider himself as a damned soul or a soul tormented by the devil in one area, but as a reincarnate in another. If Jasbir had lived in a medieval Catholic environment, would he not have been considered as a kind of obsessed? And, again, one may wonder what it was that prevented the good people of Watseka from considering Laurancy as a reincarnation of Mary Roff, if not the fact that, most probably, little or nothing was known about reincarnation in such American provincial environments at that time. Things would probably be very different today and great swarms of neo-reincarnationists would descend upon the case, bent on not letting it get away; indeed, the first to speak of reincarnation would probably be the protagonists themselves.

Whenever people speak of reincarnation, they always do so under the suggestive force of an idea that, taken by itself, seems indeed rather appealing: they are thinking of a series of lives as a chain of existences, each life being in itself finished and complete, followed by another and then yet another, and so on, like the beads of a necklace. This is very clearly brought out by the words and expressions used by the subjects interviewed by Frederick Lenz who, when asked to clarify their interior visions (and here it does not really matter whether the contents were real or hallucinatory), described the series of their incarnations in the following terms: "pearls on a string", "clear globes", each of which appears "perfect" (when all is said and done, is not sphericity the symbol that we use quite spontaneously to express the idea of perfection?). And again: "chain of lifetimes" strung together "like rosary beads".(142) And Dethlefsen is also in line with this perfectly linear vision of a chain-like succession of lives when he tells us that the hypnotic regression of his subjects is effected along the following "axis": reliving one's birth, subsequently reliving the embryonic state, going back to one's previous life, then to the one before that, eventually to return to the present time and the actual situation and to wake up again.(143) In short, he speaks of a backward and forward motion along a single track.

The fact is that the concept of reincarnation has always been of this "single-track" type, that reincarnation has always been conceived in the manner of a "string of pearls": this is so because the suggestiveness of the concept is accepted from the very beginning and then constantly reaffirmed precisely on account of the fact that it represents an extremely simple, clear and linear idea that can be readily understood and, what is more, is not devoid of a certain aesthetic beauty, a certain fascination. One may assume that reincarnationism has always had an element of autosuggestion in this direction.

A suggestion that the subject receives or in some way gives himself at the beginning will create a kind of psychic trace or rut that is destined to become deeper and deeper as the suggestion is repeated and confirmed. Gradually, therefore, as this psychic rut becomes deeper, as it is confirmed as the one and only in a process of self-absolutization, as it were, it increasingly excludes the formation of alternative wheel tracks: with all its weight, the wheel will always turn in the bottom of this rut and deviating from it becomes more and more difficult as time goes by.

This consideration, which is of a perfectly general nature, is applicable also (and above all) to the ambit of individual hypnotic regression treatments. Right from the beginning, indeed, everything in these treatments contributes to suggesting to the subject that the reincarnation process gives rise to nothing other than a succession of existences in the manner of a string of pearls: it is therefore only reasonable to expect that even if in the course of the present existence of subject B there should have occurred a series of reincarnation "impacts" (A, A', A", etc: not clamorous like the impact of Sobha Ram on Jasbir, but rather discreet and practically unperceived), the subject himself would regress under hypnosis only to A, while A', A", etc., would remain buried in his unconscious and therefore completely ignored.

In actual practice, however, one may note that, notwithstanding this dominant pattern in the traditional idea of reincarnation, the observed phenomena of the reincarnation type are often far removed from this linearity, far removed from conforming to this "pearl necklace" pattern. There are cases in which the presumed reincarnation makes itself felt in the body (or, to be more precise, in the personality) of an individual many years after his birth: at three and a half years of age, for example, in the case of Jasbir, at eight in the case of the boy designated to succeed the Lama Mé Thôn-Tsampo as abbot of the Ky-rong monastery, even though the lama had only just died. The two cases – the first personally followed by Stevenson, the second witnessed by Rivière – are both reported by Muller, as we have already noted.

Muller then describes a third case, accepting the spiritist-reincarnationist interpretation that is given to the phenomena, it would seem, by the author of the book *Essays from the Unseen*, from which Muller takes the details of the case. This book is claimed to have been written through mediums, though what is of interest for our immediate purposes is not so much whether the case is correctly reported in all its details, but rather the fact that it expresses an idea that as convinced a reincarnationist as Muller finds perfectly acceptable.

Among others, the book affirms that a certain Jan van Leyden, who lived in the sixteenth century, had lost a twin brother at a very early age and that the spirit of this twin brother had subsequently taken possession of Jan's body. And this fact, as Muller comments, "could explain why Leyden's character was later so different from that of his younger years."[144] In another passage of the same book Muller reminds us that "the possibility of a spirit taking over the body of another person, at least temporarily, is also suggested by other cases, for instance, the 'Watseka Wonder', in the U.S.A., and the Iris Farczady case in Hungary. There is also a case of astral projection, caused by an accident. The victim came to the bed of a child who had just died, and felt an urge to take possession of the little body."[145]

This brings us to cases in which an individual seems to become reincarnated not after death, as the most widespread and typical idea of reincarnation would have it, but actually prior to dying. Muller notes that Stevenson came across cases where rebirth was claimed to have occurred before the previous person had died.[146] Elsewhere, therefore, Muller actually expresses himself as follows: "There are a few cases where rebirth took place before death! We have no right to contend this is impossible. If it occurs we have to find out how it is possible."[147] Moreover, Muller affirms that he personally followed a case of this kind. The subject in question was a German by the name of Hermann Grundei, who, guided by his own intuitions, memories, etc., set out in search of his previous incarnation and eventually identified it in the person of somebody who had committed suicide in 1887, the year in which Grundei had been born. A series of objective signs, which I shall not here restate, seem in some way or other to confirm the idea that the suicide became reincarnated in the other, or at least – to remain in line with my own hypothesis – that something of the dead man, say his astral shell or some fragment thereof, succeeded in transferring itself to Grundei and becoming inglobated in this psychism. There is only one little difficulty: the supposed reincarnate was born on 19 October, while the suicide (presumed to be his previous incarnation) shot himself on 23 November, i.e. thirty-five days later.[149]

Further reflection about this group of cases, however, causes me to wonder whether, rather than saying that subject A "died" after his "rebirth" in subject B, it would not be better to say that A became reincarnated in B a certain time after the birth of the latter. Defined in this manner, cases of the Grundei type would reduce to nothing other than the previously considered cases of the Jasbir type. But I am not altogether sure that this "cutting of the Gordian knot" can really solve all the difficulties involved in cases of the Grundei type, including the cases that Muller mentions in general terms, as it were, without citing any specific ones.

If we grant that an individual can "reincarnate" before dying, we must assume that this reincarnation does not involve the whole of his psychic personality, but only a part (a peripheral one, if you wish) of his psychism, since the core of this psychism would necessarily have to remain associated with the body, if for no other reason than to assure its physical survival until the subsequent moment of death.

On the other hand, if we want to reduce cases of the Grundei pattern to cases similar to those of Jasbir or David Paladin, if we want to suppose that in all these more general cases "reincarnation" occurs only after death, then we must also conclude that this "reincarnation" makes itself felt in the existence of the "reincarnate" only some time after his birth. As we have already noted, the Druses, unlike many other reincarnationists who consider the soul to become reincarnated in the body at the moment of conception, deem reincarnation to take place at birth. And then, as we have likewise seen (at least if we want to accept Banerjee's interpretation), one could also speak of cases like that of David Paladin, where the impact of the reincarnating personality (Kandinsky) makes itself felt only in a fully adult man.

If therefore we want to reduce all the cases that have been mentioned to just a single category, we have to postulate that "reincarnation" can take place after the birth of the new person, that it can occur months or even years later. The problem that has to be faced, however, is whether such a view is compatible with the *continuity* of the individual who dies in the old personality and then becomes reincarnated in the new one.

Reincarnationists insist a great deal on this continuity. They say that, though passing from one personality to another, the individual always remains the same. The thread of the individual's inter-reincarnative existence, if I may use that expression, maintains its continuity no matter how many pearls (i.e. individual lives) it may pass through. It is quite true that at each successive existence the individual loses all recollection of his past existences; but when he dies the next time and returns to the world of spirits, he will remember the whole of his past, and sometimes recollections of previous existences can come to the surface of a person's mind even during the course of an earthly life. No matter how many different personalities in which a given individual may become incarnated in the course of time, he always maintains the continuity of his own individual life, it is always the same individual with its many lives that in the course of this chain of existences gradually perfects himself; at times there may also be regression, but he will then return to making progress again, all the time shaping his own peculiar karma. And this karma is nothing other than the result of the positive and negative actions of one and the same individual, a result that will eventually determine the quality and the condition of the lives that follow.

Now, if we conceive the individual as having this kind of continuity that is never broken, if we conceive the individual as a subject who maintains his individuality without ever losing it (at least until the moment in which, having attained supreme perfection, he will be able to merge with the absolute), one cannot but note that such a concept of individuality runs the risk of being seriously compromised by the observable modalities of certain phenomena of the reincarnation type.

Let us consider the cases in which a subject A dies and then becomes reincarnated in subject B, who at that time may have attained an age of three months, three and a half years, eight years, or any other age you like. In certain cases the impact of A on B can be so strong as to give rise even to a possession phenomenon (the term being here understood in its widest sense, including obsession as stable possession). This would be the case of Jasbir, for example. Stevenson himself admits that "accepting a paranormal interpretation of the case, it properly speaking belongs to the group known as 'prakaya pravesh' in Hindi and 'possession' in the literature of Western psychical research."[149]

Nevertheless, even though the impact may be of this type, one can hardly say that the outcome in Jasbir's case is completely in line with the phenomenology of possession. In temporary possession, indeed, one may note that once the medium has been abandoned by the spirit that has made use of its body (or by whoever may have acted in the spirit's place), one notes a certain listlessness due to the energies that had to be furnished to the spirit, sometimes the person even remains exhausted, but in every other respect the personality remains exactly what it was before.

The same may be said of people who have been victims of an obsession, no matter how long it may have lasted, once the occupying personality has gone away. But as we already had occasion to note, the case of Jasbir is rather different. Here the personality of Sobha Ram, the young Brahmin who died at the age of twenty-two, would seem to have inserted itself all of a sudden and in a manner that is altogether in line with the phenomenology of possession. Once this had happened, however, it did not remain distinct from Jasbir's own personality, as normally happens in phenomena of possession and, more particularly, obsession. The two personalities, far from merely coexisting as distinct entities, far from alternating in taking control of Jasbir's body, came to merge in the course of time, so that the final outcome was a Jasbir enriched by elements of the personality of Sobha Ram. In other words, Jasbir in the end englobed at least something of Sobha Ram's personality, he assimilated it, made it his own, in some way combined it with his own pre-existing personality. Following the development of Jasbir's personality from birth onwards, one can note a continuity that is undoubtedly thrown into a state of crisis by the irruption of Sobha Ram's personality (or some part of it), but is not broken, is not interrupted, because Jasbir eventually achieves a balanced consciousness of himself, albeit enriched by new elements and sustained by the idea (and here it does not matter whether this idea is true or false) that he had been the Brahmin Sobha Ram in a previous life.

Going now to the other pole, Sobha Ram's personality, at least as regards the elements that seem to have become "reincarnated" in Jasbir, to all appearances allowed itself to become absorbed by the personality of the boy. Following its invasion of Jasbir's personality, indeed, Sobha Ram's personality became gradually absorbed, ceased to exist as an independent personality and also as a distinct individuality. It no longer is something of its own, it no longer consists of something that is distinct from every surrounding reality, it no longer lives in continuity with itself, it breaks this continuity, what was once an individual becomes a non-individual, becomes a mere psychic formation that another individual absorbs and makes his own, becomes an integral part of the personality of another individual, almost as if it had been eaten, digested and assimilated by another person.

In other words, the personality and the very individuality of Sobha

Ram could be considered as maintaining a continuity with themselves only in case they are conceived as subsisting and persisting. But if his personality were to become dissolved in that of Jasbir, his individuality could not be considered to survive according to the traditional linear pattern of reincarnationism, for the last pearl would have merged with a pearl of another necklace and the thread would have become interrupted, would no longer subsist as an *individual* thread, as a thing in itself.

Sobha Ram would therefore have to survive himself, survive elsewhere, because on becoming reincarnated in Jasbir according to the phenomenology of that particular case he would lose his peculiar personality and his individuality. There are two possible solutions, two possible ways of interpreting the facts of the case, that would ensure the survival or persistence of both personalities: Firstly, we may consider that the true core of Sobha Ram's personality has never invaded Jasbir at all, that what has invaded the boy is nothing other than an astral residue of the personality of the young Brahmin, who – following his death – cast it off like a slough. Alternatively, one could hold that Sobha Ram has invaded Jasbir as in a case of obsession and then abandoned him, following a behaviour pattern similar to the one presumed to have been adopted by the entity "Mary Roff" vis-à-vis Laurancy Vennum (with all the analogies that, as already noted, this behaviour bears to the phenomena of being obsessed by the devil); but with one essential difference: whereas in cases of obsession the occupying entity will as a general rule abandon the occupied personality sooner or later, leaving it more or less as it was before the possession phenomenon manifested itself, in Jasbir's case the entity "Sobha Ram" abandons the occupied personality only after having left an astral slough that the boy subsequently seems to have gradually absorbed and incorporated in his own psychism.

To me, all these considerations confirm that if one can speak of a something that becomes reincarnated, that becomes transmitted from a dead person to a living one this something cannot be the nucleus of the personality or the individuality of the deceased, but only some relatively secondary or peripheral element of his psychism.

I do not in any way claim to have "demonstrated" this: all I have done is to put forward some considerations that, taken as a whole, seem to *suggest* such a proposition, just as the cases investigated by Stevenson and those summarized and classified by Muller seem *suggestive of reincarnation,* that is to say, they seem to *suggest the reincarnation,* if not of *somebody,* at least of *something.*

All considered, one can say that even though a comparative examination of the various concrete cases does not seem to confirm the assumption or proposition of the reincarnation of the essential core of the personality, the facts do seem to be sufficient to suggest, somewhat more limitedly, the reincarnation of something that we might call *psychic residues.*

CHAPTER V

Reincarnation of Psychic Residues

The more restricted view of the reincarnation process that has taken shape in these pages would seem to draw some comfort and element of confirmation from a concept put forward by René Guénon, a French traditionalist philosopher, who observes that "the dissociation that follows death involves not only the bodily elements (of the person) but also certain elements that could be described as psychic."[150] I shall not dwell on certain reasons for this phenomenon, which – especially in the form in which Guénon adduces them – do not seem to me to be particularly plausible,[151] just as certain other considerations that he connects therewith do not always seem wholly plausible, and shall go straight to his conclusions, some of which seem altogether acceptable. "Certain facts that reincarnationists think they can invoke in support of their theories can be explained perfectly well" not only "by the hereditary transmission of certain psychic elements", but also "by the assimilation into a human individuality of other psychic elements deriving from the disintegration of anterior human individualities, though the latter need not for this reason have even the least spiritual relationship with the former."[152] It may also happen "that, more or less by chance, a fairly considerable set of such elements is preserved without becoming dissociated and then transferred as a unit to a new individuality."[153] Chance events of this kind are particularly striking as far as reincarnationists are concerned and seem to support, though quite illusorily, their belief in a reincarnation that somehow or other involves the very core of the subject's individuality.

It is only too natural to connect Guénon's conclusions with those reached by Emilio Servadio in an article entitled *Natura e modalità della "Reincarnazione"* (Nature and Modalities of "Reincarnation").[154] The question that Servadio asks himself is: "*Who*, or *what*, could or should become reincarnated?" He rejects the idea that such a *quid* (or *quis* as I would add) can coincide with the soul if it is considered as a somebody or a something, that is, as a stable and permanent entity to the point where (using words that are not Servadio's) one can say that Tom, on dying, becomes reincarnated in Dick; in other words, to the point where one can say that the present Dick was Tom in a previous incarnation. A tacit identification of this kind, which in actual practice is very common among reincarnationists, founds the fallacious assumption that the personality has a permanent and indestructible nucleus, identifying it with the customary and day to day manner in which each one of us "feels" his own self (ego). We can underscore a statement already made at the beginning of this study by noting that, according to Servadio, such an identification "is contradicted by a long series of facts. The first of these facts is constituted by the infinite gamut of modifications, distortions and injuries that the aforesaid 'sense of the ego' can undergo as a result of illness, trauma or, more simply, senile deterioration. Furthermore, it is well known that the empirical ego is to a very large extent subject to internal psychological influences, the roots of which are substantially unknown on account of the fact that they are wholly unconscious. The ego, in fact, must always take account of what the unconscious parts of the psychic apparatus (known in psychoanalysis as the 'superego' and the 'es') may require (or prohibit or deform)."[154] As far as Servadio is concerned, it is precisely this situation of dependence and variability of the phenomenic ego that prevents it from representing the foundation for the assumption that there exists a permanent core of the personality of an individual that is destined to survive, an individual that is destined to become transferred from the broken-down edifice of a dying body to the new and habitable dwelling of a freshly conceived and generated body.

Let us for the moment stop at this point of the line of argument developed by this well known Italian psychoanalyst and parapsychologist and note, first of all, that he is saying something that is in complete contrast with the affirmations of certain reincarnationists who, like Resat Bayer[155] for example, sustain that the fact of reincarnation (a fact demonstrated or at least suggested by a whole series of phenomena) constitutes the sole valid proof of survival (which cannot be demonstrated in any other way, and cannot be argued with certainty even on the basis of parapsychic phenomena of the spiritist type). In sharp opposition to considerations of this kind,

Servadio seems to be saying that reincarnation of a certain type (i.e. of a permanent core of the human personality that can be defined as the ego or the soul) does not exist, and for the very reason that a certain type of immortality (i.e. an "immortality of the soul" as such, understood in the classical sense) does not exist.

I have no difficulty in agreeing that the empirical ego as such must not be attributed any substantiality, permanence, or eternity, for to the extent to which such qualities can be conceived as absolutes, they are to be attributed – essentially and originarily – only to the absolute itself. In the truest and fullest sense of the term, only God is "substance", because in the proper sense only God is "reality that does not need any other reality in order to exist".[157] Only God is therefore truly eternal, only God is everlasting.

But, one may ask, could not the finite things of this earth be made infinite in some way? Yes, indeed, but only by God, that is to say, by virtue of an initiative taken by the Infinite itself. Now, in the perspective that takes shape from the unanimous testimony of the mystics, is not man, is not the interiority of man the privileged place of the presence of God, of the manifestation of God? In spite of the earthly mud from which he is forged and notwithstanding the animal nature in which he is immersed, in spite of the sum of his imperfections and miseries, could not man have something of the divine within him, at least in the inchoate and germinal state, and this certainly not because of any originary capacity of his own, but rather because of a virtue he has derived from God? The perspective I adopt here in hypothetical form is the one that sees man as privileged creature and, in some way, as the potential incarnation of God himself.

Psychologists may study the nature of the phenomenic ego of man and explore its imperfect and labile character, but only a deeper probing into a particular metaphysico-religious experience and in line with a particular perspective (the biblical or Judaico-Christian perspective, that is) would be capable of grasping in man, seen as a whole, also the aspect of his potential absoluteness: the aspect, in other words, according to which man, though incarnated in a body and a psyche that are imperfect, labile and ephemeral, yet receives from the divine presence within him the capacity of becoming substantial, immortal, eternal, perfect, absolute.

I believe that there is only one way in which one can conceive and save the "immortality of man's soul" and thus also the "substantiality" of this soul: by not attributing it to man as such, but taking it to derive rather from a particular and privileged presence of God, a presence that is attested by the mystics and grasped in an altogether special manner by a particular metaphysical and religious experience as developed in a certain spiritual tradition.

If, therefore, the core of the human personality is preserved and survives not for its own sake, but rather by virtue of the divine presence within it that turns it into something divine in the making, then one may ask oneself whether this nucleus of the personality, over and above surviving, also becomes reincarnated.

Now, whereas the phenomenon of possession – irrespective of whether it be of short or long duration – gives one the impression of a strong presence (that later disappears very suddenly, leaving the subject to all intents and purposes as before), the cases that suggest reincarnation convey an equally clear impression that the asserted presence of a deceased (or of the nucleus of his individuality) in the personality of a "living" subject is far weaker in nature: it is quite true that the first impact may often be stronger, so much so as to provoke a crisis of the sense of identity of the receiving subject; but it is also true that this normally happens at a time when the personality of the receiving subject is extremely immature (in the years of childhood, and often even in very early infancy) or at a moment when the subject finds himself in a feverish and delirious state, often in a coma or close to it. Whereas in prolonged and stable possessions (especially in the ones we have defined as "total") the possessing subject seems to have the strength and capacity to entrench himself in the personality of the possessed and to bend it to his will, thus using it as an instrument, in the phenomena suggestive of reincarnation the possessing personality always seems to express itself in a far weaker manner and, what is more, seemingly allows itself to become absorbed by the personality of the receiving subject, which ends up by digesting and assimilating it in some way. So everything leads one to the view, at least in the cases that lend themselves more readily to being interpreted as reincarnation phenomena, that a possessing personality that has such a massive first impact and then allows itself to be so readily absorbed can be defined not as something that is still alive, as something that has survived the death of the body, but rather as a kind of psychic corpse, or even as a simple shred of such a corpse.

At this point we can come back to Servadio. "It has been quite rightly observed," he writes in the previously quoted article, "that the persistence after death of some elements or parts of corporeal life – with the successive biochemical modifications associated with gradual organic dissolution – enables one to suppose that in the greater part of cases something analogous can happen to certain elements of the 'psychic corpse' prior to its total dissolution."[158] These elements can persist either in an ephemeral manner or last for a longer period of time. In general, Servadio thinks it possible for such "portions or elements of the personality" to become reincarnated.[159]

I shall forego quoting any of the other considerations made by Servadio to complete and strengthen the line of argument I have here reported: what I am primarily interested in at this point is simply to note the idea of a possible reincarnation of "portions or elements of the personality", of "elements" of a "psychic corpse" that is about to dissolve.

It seems to me to be worthwhile to stop for a moment in order to compare this idea of reincarnation mooted by Servadio with the not altogether different idea of "rebirth" that Ian Stevenson generally attributes to Buddhism. At this point it will be useful to go back to the two definitions given by Stevenson and recalled at the very beginning of our considerations. The first of these definitions, which Stevenson refers essentially to a Hindu context, seems to express the very view of reincarnation that Servadio rejects: "The union of a soul with a new physical body after the death of the physical body with which it was previously associated." The other definition concerns "rebirth" and would undoubtedly be far more acceptable as far as Servadio is concerned: as understood in Buddhist environments, rebirth is "the activation of a new physical body by *effects* or *residues* that had previously been associated with another (now deceased) physical body".[160]

Attributing *sic et simpliciter* the first of the two ideas to Hinduism and the second to Buddhism, as Stevenson does, may seem excessively rigid and schematic. For my own part, I simply want to quote the two definitions as expressing two concepts of reincarnation – or transmigration or rebirth, or any other name one wants to give it – that are and remain wholly different from each other in all their essential and significant respects.

In a subsequent explanatory note to integrate his article, Servadio seems to accept the idea – though many others refuse and reject it – of "one's own empirical ego as something inconsistent and transitory, something that one would do well to get rid of".[161] I have already said that as far as I am concerned the ego – and let me make it clear that I mean the empirical ego – acquires consistency, perennialness and eternity, an absoluteness of its own, solely and exclusively by virtue of the presence within it of God and, more specifically, the incarnate God: that is to say, the God who does not limit himself to being present in an undifferentiated manner, but who defines and individuates himself in each one of us by giving value to and enhancing our individual characteristics, strengthening all the individual notes of his integral personality; to give but one example, strengthening within me not only the fact of my "being man" in a generic sense, but also my being wholly and integrally John Smith, with all the unique and irrepeatable personal notes that this implies at every level.

In my particular perspective – where the empirical ego is saved by the presence in it of the living, creating and incarnate God – the characteristics of transitoriness and inconsistency that Servadio attributes to the empirical and phenomenic ego as a whole have to be attributed rather to certain peripheral elements thereof, elements that the ego at times may find it desirable to shed. My particular perspective, therefore, goes not visualize the reabsorption of individuals in an undifferentiated primigenial unity, but rather fullness of life for each individual precisely on account of his individuality. Unlike Servadio's, mine is not a Vedantic perspective, but rather a clearly biblical perspective; moreover, I simply propose it to my readers without any attempt of convalidating it in these pages, which are dedicated to a very different subject matter.

The Bible's eschatological perspective destines each individual not only to the fullness of life, but to the fullness of life at every level, including the corporeal-physical level, even though the corporeity in question has to be perfectly spiritualized and turned into a vehicle of the loftiest spirituality: it is not by chance that the Bible speaks of "resurrection" (however this term may have to be understood).

Although destined to the fullness of life at every level, and therefore to resurrection (however one may want to conceive it), it may be that in a particular situation – on the occasion of bodily death, say, or at some time after – the individual may have to free himself of certain psychic dross, free himself of certain psychic appendages that served him in good stead for as long as he was living at a certain level and no longer serve him to subsist – as it were – at a different vibratory level. All these considerations seem to suggest that it may well be this psychic dross, these peripheral elements of the human personality that eventually become reincarnated.

Annie Besant, in her little book entitled *Death – and after?*[162], summarizes what is generally considered to be the thought of theosophists about the *post-mortem* condition and writes that man throws off not only his physical body but also the "etheric double" to enter into an intermediate state, known as Kamaloka, from which he subsequently issues by shedding a third body, the "shell" or "desire body".

Shedding of the first two bodies coincides with death in the proper sense of the term, while the shedding of the third body is the "second death". The physical body, the etheric double and the shell, each at its own level and in its own peculiar manner, are all destined to disintegrate. The elements into which these bodies dissolve subsequently become recycled at their respective levels of existence and vibration. And, just as the molecules of matter enter into ever new chemical syntheses in the material world, so also may one expect and imagine the psychic elements to become continuously recycled within the ambit of the psychic universe. Because the psychic entities of the living incarnates continue to subsist at the vibratory level abandoned by the disincarnate, one may also expect that the psychic residues cast off by the deceased will attach themselves to the psychisms of the living incarnates, to what constitutes the psychic dimension of each. Furthermore, one may expect the destination of the psychic residues abandoned by a deceased (i.e. the fact that they become "reincarnated" in the psychic dimension of a particular living incarnate rather than in that of another) to be determined *by affinity,* i.e. by the law of affinity that is suggested by the convergence of many different phenomena and is said to be the true law of the gravitation of souls, the law that regulates all mutual attraction between psychic entities and realities, between all the components of the psychic and spiritual universe.

That the psychic corpses abandoned by souls as they ascend to higher levels can become conserved for a certain period of time or, rather, that they tend to be conserved for as long as possible, is a phenomenon that can already be deduced from every expression of life in our own material world, where every living being, even the most harmful germs and all illness and disease, tend to become conserved and thus to expand and perpetuate themselves to the greatest possible extent

Even though she does so in a context that has little or nothing to do with our present discussion, Annie Besant briefly mentions a certain type of psychic entity that has become separated from the centre of the personality to which it was attached and has shed also the physical body and the etheric double: adhering only to the "desire body", this psychic entity, though it has ceased to convey and express any form of human life that could be understood as such, seeks to survive at all costs, even though – like the germs of an illness or the berserk cells of a tumour – it may by that time be moving in a wholly negative direction. This autonomous psychic reality "lives for a while, for a longer or shorter time according to the vigour of its vitality, a wholly evil thing, dangerous and malignant, seeking to renew its fading vitality by any means laid open to it by the folly or ignorance of still embodied souls. Its ultimate fate is, indeed, destruction, but it may work much evil on its way to self-chosen doom".[163]

In this connection it is interesting to note an affirmation made by Annie Besant, and also by theosophists in general, that one finds cropping up again in Guénon (even though one may contest the exclusive character that this statement seems to arrogate itself); it concerns the astral "shells" that manifest themselves during medianic séances: "Many of the responses to eager enquiries at *séances* come from such 'Shells', drawn to the neighbourhood of friends and relatives by the magnetic attractions so long familiar and dear, and automatically responding to the waves of emotion and remembrance, to the impulse of which they had so often answered during the lately closed earth-life. Phrases of affection, moral platitudes, memories of past events, will be all the communications such 'Shells' can make, but these may literally pour out under favourable conditions under the magnetic stimuli freely applied by the embodied friends and relatives."[164]

This interpretation has numerous points of contact with a hypothesis that seems to have been formulated for the first time about a century ago Adolphe D'Assier.[165] As Bozzano tells us, D'Assier, a convinced materialist, happened one day to witness some complex phenomena of infestation, so that he posed himself the problem of formulating an explanation that he could reconcile with his materialist view of reality, which excluded the idea of survival. He thus put forward a hypothesis, according to which – if I may here use the words that Bozzano employs to summarize the theory – there "survives only, and for a very short time, an ephemeral 'posthumous phantasm', a kind of 'spectre from beyond the tomb', which for some time retains a certain vitality and a vague feeling of existing; and for this reason it is attracted towards environments where there are mediums in trance". Merging with the medium's perispirit, it thus acquires a certain, though temporary consciousness of itself, giving rise to the manifestations – which the author deems always to be rudimental – of the so-called spirits of the dead. Nevertheless, this miserable remnant of the human personality, exposed as it is to luminous, calorific and electric vibrations, is subject to rapid disintegregation and becomes completely dissipated within a brief period of time."[166]

Bozzano notes that D'Assier's theory has also been adopted, subject only to some very slight modifications, by Broad. There has thus taken shape the hypothesis of the "psychic factor", although (as Bozzano goes on to say) even this proves inadequate to explain *all* the metapsychic phenomena, some of which – he holds – can be interpreted only on the basis of spiritist assumptions, namely the view that these phenomena are due to the direct intervention of the deceased themselves. But the theories of D'Assier and Broad remain interesting in connection with the particular interpretation we have here adopted in considering reincarnation phenomena.

Servadio, too, agrees in identifying the presumed communicating "spirits" with psychic shreds and tatters that the more ingenious spiritists mistake for the true, consistent, coherent and integral personalities of the deceased.[167]

Turning now to more recent days, considerable interest has been attached to a conclusion that is said to have been reached by Denys Kelsey, an English psychiatrist, even though his researches seem to aim in a very different direction. Let me therefore refer to his work and views in the terms in which they are reported by Ugo Dèttore.

Kelsey, assisted by his wife Joan Grant (who is endowed with considerable sensitive faculties), has concerned himself with cases of neuroses thought to be caused by psychic trauma suffered by the subject in a previous life. A good example is provided by the case of a young man, who – though tall and strong – was obsessed by the idea that there was something effeminate in the shape of his hips. On subjecting the patient to hypnotic treatment, slowly there emerged a story set in a supposed previous life of the young man, in which – to say it somewhat improperly – he had been a girl who, after having been seduced and abandoned, died as a result of an attempt to procure abortion. I use the term "improperly" because, if I may paraphrase Kelsey's conclusion, it had been the circumstances of this death, in the grips of fear and in solitude, to cause *an element of her personality to dissociate* and to become frozen in a present, out of time as it were; *the integrated components became reincarnated* within two years, but in a male body.[168]

Ugo Dèttore points out that in this manner Kelsey proposes a possible variant of the theory of reincarnation, holding it *to be possible for reincarnation not to involve the whole personality, but only some of its psychic components* that first become dissociated and subsequently enter (and thus come to form part of) another living being.[169]

For those anxious to know the sequel of the story, let me add that the young man, apprised of the antecedents that had emerged from the hypnotic treatment, freed himself of the obsessive idea and was thus cured in a single session, seemingly as a result of nothing other than this new-found awareness of the antecedents.

Summarizing, then, the personality of a human being can thus be said to be a subdivided whole, made up of parts that, little by little, can detach themselves. Not only the physical body, therefore, but also peripheral elements of the psyche can detach themselves sooner or later from the core of the human personality, somewhat in the manner of sloughs. And it is precisely these psychic fragments that eventually become reincarnated: made to exist only at a certain vibratory level, they are thought to be no longer capable of following the soul when, after having become fully and definitively disincarnate, it ascends to a higher level of more subtle vibrations.

One can quite readily understand that these astral residues, floating in the occult environment closest to the earth, can in the end become attracted – as a result of affinity – by the psychisms of men still living on the earth. These psychisms would still be constituted in such a way as to be able to subsist and animate bodies at the low vibratory level, i.e. they would still be constituted in a manner altogether similar to these astral residues, so much so that they can easily interact with them; and this means that they can attract them, be possessed by them (and possibly also managed by them to a certain extent), and ultimately englobe them.

The idea I am gradually outlining and defining here has also been expressed, albeit in a somewhat different and complementary manner, in a book by Jane Roberts, another well known American author and psychic. She takes the view that the personal identity of each one of us is integrally maintained, although there can be interactions at the level of what she calls the "peripheries" of each personality.[170] Interaction and exchange: fragments of the consciousness of an individual can become detached and be used by others, although the original subject continues to maintain his own identity. The experiences made by each one of us, though remaining personal and private, come to form part of a kind of psychic bank of the human species and are available drawn on by others; every man or woman can therefore draw something from this bank not only before being born, but also at any time during his life: "In some cases you change so much that people knowing you at different times would seem to know and describe entirely different people.The theory of reincarnation is an attempt to see the basic, inviolate, yet many-faceted self in terms that can be understood, and that are in keeping with popular concepts of time . . . You are actually 'reincarnated' many times in one lifetime."[171]

Let us now take another step forward in developing our line of argument by noting that certain phenomena that occur during séances can be defined as possessions quite irrespective of whether the possessing entity is a true subject, a deceased, or simply an astral shell. An astral shell, indeed, would be nothing other than a slough that a deceased has cast off in order to make it possible for him to become integrated at a level of higher or subtler vibrations, where this shell, precisely on account of its denser and more material nature, would constitute more of a hindrance than a help. One could therefore speak of *possessions brought about* either *by a deceased* or by *an astral shell*.

Since we are concerned with possessions, however, it will be as well to remember the very considerable difference that there may be between a *temporary possession of a medium,* such as may occur during the course of a séance and a *prolonged medianic possession,* which can arise also outside a session and continue for several days, weeks, months, and even years. Let us assume therefore that there can be *prolonged medianic possessions* brought about either by a *deceased* or by an *astral shell.*

Having made this fourfold distinction, let us now turn our attention to the first two terms and ask ourselves whether and in what manner it is possible to discern whether a temporary possession, occurring during a séance, is brought about by a deceased, i.e. a true disincarnate subject, or by a mere astral shell. I think that here it is far more difficult to give an answer than in the case of possessions that continue for months or even years.

An astral shell can express itself like the unconscious of a person in a state of deep hypnosis, with the same intelligence and the same creativity. From the intellectual point of view, therefore, it is not possible to decide with certainty whether the medium is possessed by a deceased who is expressing himself in full consciousness or by an astral shell that preserves the memory of the entity from which it has become detached and is therefore equally capable of expressing itself in the manner characteristic of that entity's personality.

Nor would it be possible to distinguish the manifestations of astral shells on account of a lesser "force" they display as compared with the manifestations of disincarnate subjects in the proper sense of the term. As compared with the latter, indeed, the force of astral shells could well be integrally preserved for a certain period of time and become attenuated only at a later stage as these shells gradually dissolve. Consequently, if the séance were to be held during the initial period in which the ethereal shell preserves its force more or less intact, the manifestations of such shells would not differ very greatly from the corresponding manifestations of true transcendental personalities as far as the energy and vitality aspect is concerned.

A far clearer and more visible difference may however be revealed in cases where the possession continues for a certain period of time. A personality in the proper sense of the term, i.e. the disincarnate personality of a deceased, will maintain itself integral and well defined even in the course of time, so that it will appear clearly distinct from everything other than itself and therefore fully determinate. For this reason, if a true disincarnate personality comes to occupy for a long period of time the personality of a man or woman still living incarnate on this earth, it can happen that sooner or later it will abandon the possessed personality. After such an abandonment the former occupying personality will come to be once more fully itself.

The same may be said of the man or woman who was occupied by it and has now regained complete freedom: just like a medium returns to being himself at the end of a séance in which he has lent his body to one or more disincarnate entities, so also a man (or woman) who has been possessed for a long period of time by one or more such entities will return into possession of his normal personality after the abandonment and will therefore once again display his former characteristic ways of thinking, speaking and acting.

But what happens in cases where an astral shell invades and occupies a "living" person for a long time? It may well happen at first that the shell will forcefully dominate the occupied personality, so much so that the latter may even lose the sense of its identity, i.e. the subject will no longer consider himself to be John Smith, as he was before becoming possessed, but rather Dick Jones or whatever else may have been the name of the occupying entity. This situation of dependence on the occupying entity, this feeling of even being the occupying entity and complete oblivion of one's own personal identity, can be facilitated when the occupied subject finds himself in a phase in which his personality is not yet fully formed (as in early childhood, for example) or when he is passing through a grave crisis. There can be no doubt as to the vital force and psychic consistency that astral shells can manifest immediately after detachment and during the early states of their autonomous existence. But this consistency and force seem destined to become gradually attenuated in the course of time.

Those who seem to speak of these things with a certain competence – occultists, clairvoyants, communicating dead, and so on – agree in saying that astral shells are nothing other than dross or residues destined to complete disintegration. If one assumes that affinity can lead these residues to become incorporated in men and women still living on this earth, one may also expect that, even though the first impact may be very strong (by virtue of the force of the shell and the weakness of the receiving subject), the astral residues will subsequently weaken and that this will sometimes be accompanied by a gradual strengthening of the host personality: in situations of this kind one can therefore very readily understand that the shells, the astral dross or residues, precisely because they gradually weaken and tend to disintegrate within the host personality, will eventually be absorbed by that personality, which will assimilate them to the point where they become totally merged with it.

One might also expect that, together with the residues of the absorbed personality, some of its memories and recollections will eventually become integrated in the other personality so that the latter, on being subjected to hypnotic regression, will give expression to these recollections as if they were its own: this could provide an explanation of the regressions that bring out authentic contents, and which are very different from the ones that limit themselves to bringing to the surface mere unconscious re-elaborations of experiences made during the present life.

By way of hypothesis, one could also say that the impact of an astral shell on an incarnate personality is likely to be all the greater, and therefore also more noticeable, if the shell is still a single unit and not yet dispersed into fragments: if the disintegration is a process that begins at once (i.e. at the very moment when the astral shell first becomes detached from the personality to which it belonged), one may assume that what becomes incarnated in men and women still living on the earth is sometimes a shell that is still united (and these would be the cases in which the impact is more evident from outside), while in other cases it could be a simple fragment of a shell that has already disintegrated, so that parts of it are also to be found elsewhere. In such cases the part would contain the whole – as is only in the logic of the living – and each fragment would therefore bring with it the recollections of the entire astral shell and therefore of the personality from which the shell derives. On this assumption it would thus be possible for various astral or psychic fragments of the same deceased person to become reincarnated in different human personalities.

A reincarnation conceived in this manner comes rather close to the model suggested by Servadio (which he deems to be valid at least for the vast majority of cases, if not for all).

When concerned with medianic possessions of short duration (i.e. not more than a séance), it may sometimes be difficult to decide whether the possessing entity is true personality or merely an astral shell cast off by a disincarnate personality. But when the medium is possessed for a long period of time, the distinction is likely to become easier and more certain: in the long run, indeed, one will probably be able to decide with ever greater certainty whether the occupant is a true personality (and therefore displays a vitality that always maintains itself at the same level) or a mere psychic residue that becomes ever more evanescent and, so it would seem, increasingly absorbed by the personality it has come to occupy.

These cases in which a medium is possessed for a long period of time by a psychic residue could be considered as cases of "reincarnation", though obviously in the more limited sense previously defined. As such, these "reincarnation" cases, where the possessing entity is a simple astral residue that is destined to become gradually absorbed, could be distinguished ever more clearly and sharply from cases of "obsession", where (as we have already explained in some detail) the possessing entity seems to be a true human subject.

In a "reincarnation" conceived in this manner the only true continuity is the one between an individual subject and himself: the personality that is born and then continues even after physical death (and then – it would seem – even after possible subsequent astral deaths) is one and the same personality that evolves along a line that knows no interruption. Other personalities may give something of their own to this personality we are here considering (i.e. the psychic residues they leave behind in their ascent), but they can never give themselves, they can never give anything essential to their make-up, nothing that constitutes their essential core.

In the proper sense of the term, therefore no personality ever flows into any other. Nevertheless, each individual personality can become enriched by what other personalities have made of themselves: every personality models itself and its own psyche, models its own astral shell; and once the astral residues of a disincarnate personality have become separated and attached to another personality, the latter incorporates within itself also the fruit of the actions of the former, which can be either positive or negative; and there can be no doubt that the transmitted positive psychic residues of the disincarnate personality cannot but enrich the living personality, while the transmission of negative actions must have the opposite effect and act as ballast. Given the law of affinity that governs the mental universe, one may also assume that the psychic residues abandoned during the ascent of a disincarnate soul are transmitted to an incarnate soul that is bound to it by some affinity.

At this point some readers may ask whether the idea that what becomes reincarnated is not the soul as such but the fruit of its actions, i.e. what in a certain type of oriental spirituality is called the *karman*, is not a restatement of a Buddhist concept. The concept would undoubtedly seem to coincide more or less with the Buddhist one, even though my particular perspective puts it in a rather different framework.

My perspective is of a more biblical or Judaico-Christian type. And in this connection I should like to draw attention to the fact that my view of reincarnation not only respects the continuity of development of each personality, but also shows how each personality – through the fruit of its actions and thoughts – can either help other personalities to progress or, alternately, be a cause of impediment and regression for them.

Let me be more explicit. In the view of reincarnation that I have here argued and developed, Tom always remains himself, he does not become first Dick and then Harry, although he can radiate to them the positive or negative vibrations of his very thoughts; likewise, though always invisibly, after his physical death he can transmit to Dick and Harry, together with one of his psychic residues, the positive or negative fruit of his deeds and even his thoughts.

Indeed, I am wondering whether this way of conceiving reincarnation could not represent a modest stepping-stone between the Buddhist idea of "rebirth" and the Christian concept of the "communion of the saints".

CHAPTER VI

What About Presumed Messages From The Dead?

The phenomena of the reincarnation type seem to suggest the reincarnation not of the central core of the personality, but rather of some peripheral element thereof, some astral or psychic shell or residue: in putting forward this idea, I have tried to sustain and convalidate it as best as I could, at times drawing some element of support or confirmation also from points of view related in various ways to the topic of immediate interest, views that, though often emerging from the background of different perspectives, yet have in common the particular manner of conceiving reincarnation that I have summarized here.

So far I have taken these elements in support of my thesis from a certain phenomenology that, given a minimum of good will, is quite readily accessible to us men still living incarnate in this earthly dimension. The phenomenology in question consists of the phenomena of the reincarnation type as they can be observed from the viewpoint of somebody living on this bank of existence, somebody who has not yet crossed the river. And therefore the doctrines, the theories and hypotheses I have called in support are all interpretations formulated by men who are – or were at the time – still living in our dimension. At this point, therefore, one may well ask oneself the following question: Assuming that authentic messages can be sent to us by disincarnate souls, what indications in support of this assumption reach up from this other dimension?

In other words, I want to ask myself what confirmation the particular interpretation of phenomena of the reincarnation type that I have here developed receives from what seems to be testified in this connection by messages supposedly sent by deceased persons. To what extent is my proposition confirmed, to what extent is it confuted, to what extent can it be reconciled. Let me stress, however, that I am referring only to such "transcendental" communications as, by both nature and content, are capable of inducing reasonable, level-headed and unprejudiced scholars to take them into consideration.

As regards the conditions of life in the spiritual world, the more reliable of these communications from "beyond" agree to such an extent as to provide real food for thought and to lead one to conclude that they must somehow bear witness to a common experience. When testimonies agree with each other, this generally suggests that they are reliable, at least substantially so: this is as true for the judge as it is for the historian.

It is quite true that there are certain discrepancies in the messages of the deceased. Nevertheless, even these divergences seem to be capable of being explained in one way or another, especially if one bears in mind the fact that the experiences of individual deceased can vary according to their particular spiritual state and the different levels of realization they may have attained.

A very significant feature that invariably emerges is that the "beyond" is a mental world, something that in certain respects is similar to the world of our dreams. Our dream world seems to be constituted by realities that we are accustomed to perceiving in the course of our waking life. Psychology also studies and concerns itself with the so-called "shared dreams": these are very rare experiences (or, at least, they appear such to our very limited capacities for remembering and recording them), but they do occur; and if we want to consider *post mortem* experience as oneiric and/or hallucinatory at least in certain respects, we can liken to shared dreams the experiences in which several deceased come to find themselves in the same condition and also in the same spiritual environment. It is therefore the mental patrimony of ideas, beliefs, experiences, memories and aspirations (and – if you like – also obsessions, regrets, feelings of guilt, etc.) that determines the formation of the set of mental images and forms that constitute the beyond of each particular deceased.

This mental world has at least an apparent consistency, in just the same way as this is the case of our dream world: for the world of our dreams, at least as long as the illusion lasts, seems to us to be no less real and – let us say – no less solid than the world we experience during our waking life. And yet every oneiric environment is the ideoplastic creation of the individual subject: it is the mind of the subject that shapes it by means of a process that involves, above all, the unconscious. This ideoplasty, this mental creation of images, is a phenomenon that becomes particularly important in parapsychology. Indeed, I hold that all parapsychologic phenomena are essentially ideoplastic.

This ideoplasty ends up by having effects also at the material level, where it manifests itself in the form of phenomena of various kinds (and yet always attributable to this principle, including dermographism and stigmata, wound healing and natural reconstitution of tissues, ectoplasmies and elaboration of photographable thought forms, etc.).

It is also due to an ideoplastic phenomenon that a human "projector" achieves a state of bilocation and can therefore see himself in and identify himself with a "double" in human form that has the same lineaments as his physical face and the same exterior characteristics of the physical body from which it has become temporarily detached, for it is the projector himself who forges his own "phantasm" by means of a mental creation process that, taken on the whole, is both involuntary and unconscious and, at the same time, conditioned by the subject's mental habits and his particular way of feeling himself: the "phantasm" thus appears with the subject's own lineaments and somatic characters and is also "dressed" in his customary wear. And it is precisely in this way that the subject appears to himself and possibly also to others: to sensitive mediums, above all, but in certain conditions also to the naked eye of people who are not sensitive at all, and even to the objective of a photographic camera.

All these ideoplastic creations, which take shape as a result of a spontaneous and in most cases unconscious activity of the psyche, can be modified by conscious thought, which is equally creative and can therefore give rise to other ideoplastic creations at will and without limits (at least in general principle, always provided that no special inhibiting factors come into play).

The mental environment of the beyond would seem to be very real and tangible to spirits, at least to those who comply with certain conditions that correspond to their state and have not become aware of the hallucinatory character of the experiences they are undergoing at that moment. On the other hand, one and the same environment assumes the forms that are conferred upon it by the thought of the subjects that form part of this environment and co-operate in constituting it. Since elaboration of these thought forms is conditioned by the opinions, the convictions and the beliefs of the subjects that co-create the spiritual environment in which they are gathered together as constituting an affinity group, it follows that the deceased "see" the environment as confirming things in which they had already believed for a long time. And not only do they see these things translated into realities, not only do they see them as if they were true and real, but they also see them in more or less the same way: and it is for this reason that defined spirits who find themselves grouped together in one and the same environment will inevitably end up by confirming to each other things that, even though they may seem to them to be real and objective, could well be nothing other than subjective thought forms generated by means of psychic creation and conditioned by opinions and beliefs that these subjects already professed when they lived on earth.

Let us try to illustrate what we have just said by quoting some examples of presumed communications from the dead chosen from among those that appear more credible. The four questions and answers that follow have all been taken from Arthur Findlay's book *On the Edge of the Etheric.*[172]

First interview excerpt: *Question:* "Is your world, then, a real and tangible world?" *Answer:* "Yes, it is very real to us, but the conditions in which we find ourselves depend on the condition of our mind. If we wish it we can be surrounded by beautiful country. Our mind plays a large part in our life here. Just as we live in surroundings suitable to our mental development, so we also attract to ourselves minds of the same type as our own. Like attracts like in this world."[173]

I quote these interviews by way of example, but also because they are very typical and have been chosen from among innumerable others that say substantially the same things. Here, then, is the second quotation, again taken from Findlay's book: "Our world is not material but it is real for all that, it is tangible, composed of substance in a much higher state of vibration than the matter which makes up your world. Our minds can, therefore, play upon it in a different way than yours can on the material of your world. As our mind is, so is our state. To the good their surroundings are beautiful, to the bad the reverse."[174]

Third quotation from the same book: *Question:* "Does each of you ... live in a world of your own?" *Answer:* "Everyone does, you do and so do I, but if you mean can each of us see and feel the same things, I answer, Yes. All in the same plane can sense the same things."[175]

Here is the fourth and last example: "Our thoughts and actions ...

here on earth are building for us our place in the hereafter. How many of us realize that thoughts are lasting things, and will be our companions, to influence us in an even greater degree then than now. When separated from the physical body they assume shape and form more potent for good and evil than when clothed by the earthly body."(176)

Let us now consider a part of a communication of different origin that confirms and integrates the things already said in the previous four quotations. This particular testimony about the spiritual world was given to "Cerchio Firenze 77", a Florentine spiritualist group: "One must not forego saying something about the region of the mental plane that corresponds to the heaven described by the religions, even though it be only a brief mention as in the case of the other things we have spoken about. But one has to bear in mind that a creature finding himself in this heaven would not be divided from others unless it be by a particular state of consciousness. Everything is around you. If a man has lived in such a way as to merit an eternal reward or has dedicated the whole of his life to an ideal, after passing into the plane of the mind he will – by virtue of the karma – see and experience the ideal he dreamed about. This state therefore corresponds to a state of satisfaction, of beatitude. Many entities that come forward in certain encounters come from this very region of the mental world. And this is the reason why they describe a 'beyond' similar to the one they thought existed while they were alive, because they are experiencing it and for them it is something very real, not a dream."(177)

And now three quotations from the *Letters from a Living Dead Man,* a book supposedly dictated by the disincarnate personality of an American judge, a certain David P. Hatch, who died in 1912 and manifested himself almost immediately afterwards for a period of eleven months, writing through the mediumship and hands of Elsa Barker. The entity presumed to be Judge Hatch explained things to itself and others as follows: "In this form of matter where I am men are living principally a subjective life, as men on earth live principally an objective life. These people here, being in the subjective, reason from the premises already given them during their objective on earth existence. That is why most of those who last lived in the so-called Western lands, where the idea of rhythm or rebirth is unpopular, came out here with the fixed idea that they would not go back into earth life. Hence most of them still reason from that premise."(178)

Before passing on to the next declaration made by "Judge Hatch", however, I should like to quote something said by another entity and reported in *La crisi della morte* (The Crisis of Death) by Ernesto Bozzano: "There are many questions about which we do not hold by any means the same opinion here."[179]

And now back to the late David P. Hatch from California: "The holders of different opinions on religion," he says, "are often hot in their arguments. Coming here with the same beliefs they had on earth, and being able to visualize their ideals and actually to experience the things they are expecting, two men who hold opposite creeds forcibly are each more intolerant than ever before."[180]

It would also be interesting to stop for a moment to consider the consistence that, as far as a deceased is concerned, may attach not only to his own thoughts (especially those matured during the course of his earthly existence) but also to the thoughts of others.

In this connection I should like to quote a passage from the communications that the presumed entity "Frederick Myers" made in writing through the hand of Geraldine Cummins. As can readily be seen, what "Myers" tells us really falls into the context of a different problem, namely the question whether and how it is possible for a deceased to communicate something that corresponds faithfully to his own thoughts and does not reflect the contaminations deriving from the interference of the thoughts of others; nevertheless, what "Myers" is saying is also relevant to what I want to say about the *consistence* of all these thoughts: "There is continual interpenetration of thought between the visible and invisible worlds," says the entity "Myers", "and that is what makes communication with you all the more difficult. If we could separate and classify the vast accumulation of floating thought from the living and the dead it would be far more easy then, with the way clear, to send you one easy flow of thought from one individual discarnate mind. It is possible to get lost in the vast forest of man's fancies, more particularly when you go out as a discarnate explorer. You are pretty sure to pick up false trails and in the end to give up the soluble problem in disgust. I speak not alone of minds but of the continual currents of thought thrown out by such millions tossed through our mighty Mother, the Universe, whose illimitable womb harbours them all."[181] Almost as if to conclude, "Myers" then adds: "I beg of you to remember that I am but a fallible shade."[182]

Not being infallible means that one can also be mistaken. Even

Muller speaks of "ignorant spirits" that give rise to obsession, for example, "acting from ignorance" and without "understanding their condition".[183] This leads one to think that there could also be cases in which a spirit not only professes some idea of reincarnation that does not correspond to the facts, but that he may even mistakenly think himself to be reincarnated.

Let us simply postulate all this as something that, in general principle, constitutes a possibility and for the moment turn our attention to what the presumed communicating spirits themselves have to say about reincarnation. One can readily understand the difficulty of carrying out a census in the world of spirits, or even attempting mere estimates. One may note, however, that by virtue of the law of affinity the spirits that communicate with "living" men who believe in reincarnation, at least as a general rule, will themselves be reincarnationists.

It is undoubtedly easier to draw up approximate estimates of the living receivers of such communications. Now, spiritists in the Latin countries are generally of a Kardechian stamp and base themselves on Allan Kardec's reincarnationism; spiritists in the Anglo-Saxon countries, on the other hand, are divided, about two thirds seem to be anti-reincarnationists, while the remaining third appears to accept the traditional reincarnationist doctrine. This appreciation is due to Ernesto Bozzano,[184] while Giorgio di Simone explains that the idea of reincarnation, accepted in almost all the Latin countries, has been rejected or, at least, ignored in the Anglo-Saxon countries, and that "only during the last few years, thanks to the efforts made by the International Congresses of Spiritism, the resistance of the Anglo-Saxons to the idea of reincarnation has tended to attenuate".[185]

The congresses in question, obviously, assemble not spirits but men living on this planet, among whom, evidently, ground has recently been gained by an idea regarding matters that, strictly speaking, are outside their experience; that this is so is well brought out by the fact that even Giorgio di Simone goes on to say that "proof of reincarnation is obviously very difficult to provide, or even altogether impossible, if one prescinds from the communicating 'spirits'".[186]

Apart from the cases *suggestive of reincarnation,* which I deem capable of being interpreted also by my formula of a reincarnation limited to psychic residues and in which there is nothing that obliges us to invoke traditional reincarnationist doctrines, it seems to me that we humans know very little about reincarnation as a result of our direct experience; but then, reading the lines that immediately follow the words of Bozzano that I have just quoted, I there find a consideration that seems to me to be highly significant, especially when one bears in mind that it is formulated by a scholar who is far from opposed to the idea of reincarnation. Indeed, Bozzano notes – and he has gone on record with similar statements in earlier works – that the fundamental contrast between the opinions of reincarnationists and anti-reincarnationists is "hinged on a question that is insoluble for those who debate it" and is therefore "quite meaningless, seeing that *even the communicating spirits themselves admit that they know nothing about it at all* and are simply judging matters according to their own personal aspirations".(187)

Another passage from Findlay's interviews with communicant spirits would seem to provide quite specific confirmation of what Bozzano is saying: *Question:* "Do we reincarnate again on earth?" *Answer:* "Now that is a question I find difficulty in answering. I have known no one who has. I passed over many years ago, and I have round about me those who lived thousands of years ago on earth. That is all I can say, because my knowledge does not permit me to say more."(188)

Let us go back for a moment to the letters of "Judge Hatch": "Most of the men and women here do not know that they have lived many times in the flesh. They remember their latest life more or less vividly, but all before that seems like a dream."(189) And again: "Many out here have no more memory of their former lives, before the last one, than they had while in the body."(190)

"Judge Hatch" is clearly a convinced reincarnationist. The same may be said of his little friend "Lionel", a young boy longing to reincarnate; but "Lionel" remembers that he was introduced to the reincarnationist idea by one of his schoolteachers, and the judge clearly gives the impression of having had a theosophic formation in his life or, at least, to have been affected by cultural influences of this kind. This would also seem to be the case, for example, of "Entity A", whose communications are extensively reported and commented in Giorgio di Simone's books *Rapporto dalla Dimensione X* (Report from Dimension X), *Il Cristo vero* (The True Christ), and *Dialoghi con la Dimensione X* (Dialogues with Dimension X).(191)

These conflicts of opinion that are presumed to exist even among the deceased could be explained on the basis of animist principles, which reduce all phenomena, including those of a more markedly spiritoid nature, to something that remains confined to the psyche of the so-called medium. Each group, be it reincarnationist or anti-reincarnationist, would thus have their own "spirits", which animists regard as nothing other than an expression of the psychisms of the particular "living" human individuals involved. There are undoubtedly many phenomena of an apparently spiritoid type that are much better explained by the animist hypothesis, and this even in cases where a spontaneous spiritist interpretation subsequently proved weak or inadequate.

In many cases the animist hypothesis does indeed prove to be the most critical; but if we really want to be critical and give proof of the complete lack of prejudice that befits a true critic, we have to admit that, applied to certain other phenomena, the animist interpretation proves to be so complicated and over-elaborate as to become clearly untenable. In these cases the spiritist hypothesis appears not only the simpler, but also easily the more reasonable explanation. Even though on first impact the spiritist hypothesis may prove more traumatic for our mentality (with its anthromorphisms, etc.), it will subsequently reveal itself to be more plausible for anybody prepared to admit that the anthromorphic representation that the spirits give us of the beyond, at least in the first spheres, in the first stages, can be explained only on the assumption that the *post mortem* condition is of an essentially mental character and is dominated in these early stages by the forms of ideoplasty that, as we saw earlier, are largely conditioned in their turn by the earthly images and recollections and the mental habits that the newly deceased bring with them from the earth.

The various observations made above make me feel fully authorized to view the spiritist hypothesis at least as a hypothesis to be taken into consideration. Furthermore, I consider that, likewise for the purposes of a working hypothesis, I can also assume the substantial validity of the "communications" that I have mentioned, at least the ones that seem more reliable, though always bearing in mind the possibility that they may to some extent express oneiric or hallucinatory experiences, that is to say, a kind of symbolic disguise of perceptions that are yet real in their substance.

Considered in this light, therefore, it would seem that the division into reincarnationists and non-reincarnationists is to be found even among the deceased who – by virtue of the law of affinity – succeed in communicating in a wholly natural and spontaneous manner with, respectively, groups of "living" reincarnationists (Latins for the most part) and non-reincarnationists (the majority of the Anglo-Saxons).

That deceased reincarnationist and non-reincarnationist should be in touch with living individuals holding the same opinion is to be attributed not only to this law of affinity, but also to another factor: if the reincarnationism or otherwise of a deceased derives to such a large extent from the opinions that he himself professed in this connection when he lived in our world and if the communications between the two worlds make it possible for old friendships to be maintained, thus overcoming the barrier of death, it is also natural that the contacts between deceased and living groups should follow the pattern of the old bonds that already existed between these subjects when all of them were living on the earth.

Now that we have noted not only the opinions of many deceased in the matter of reincarnation but also certain testimonies of reincarnation experiences subjectively lived in a particularly intense and dramatic manner, we can return to the hypothesis that we have here sought to formulate, develop and sustain, namely the proposition that what effectively becomes reincarnated is not the core or nucleus of the personality of the deceased, but rather a mere astral shell or fragment that he leaves behind as he evolves and becomes refined.

The implicit assumption underlying this proposition is that not only the physical body, but also the psyche (which survives the death of the physical body) is something that is of an organic nature, something that – among others – can be subdivided into a core and a periphery. In this part of our study we shall therefore try to see what could be the point of view of disincarnate entities in connection with questions that we have already discussed by reviewing the interpretations given by men living on this earth. Let us turn, first of all, to the entity "Myers" for an explanation – and to me it seems a rather good one – of this concept of the subdivision of the psyche into a core and a periphery, an explanation given with the help of a very suggestive metaphor: "Now," says 'Myers' "can – you imagine a country, take England for example, dotted over with towns all self-contained, yet looking to that vast city London for general directions and for certain essential stimulus? Such is the condition of the discarnate being. He is a kingdom, bounded by what would seem to have the appearance of a veil. It has a curious elasticity. I mean, we differ from the kingdom to which I have alluded in that we can alter at will the shape of this very subtle material or fluid."(192)

One can readily understand that a province of this kingdom, even though it already possessed considerable autonomy when it still formed an integral part of the realm, will be able to act with even greater autonomy after it has become detached and independent. This is precisely what seems to happen in the case of the "old cloak" or "after-image" that, as we have just seen, "Myers" talks about. Indeed, "Myers" tells us that these shells "might be likened to an old traveller's cloak. Though he discards it, it remains by the roadside and may be picked up and worn again".(193)

As a general rule, it would seem that these "abandoned shells" are responsible for the so-called infestation phenomena. Subject to some exceptions, as "Myers" goes on to tell us, when faced with phenomena of this type we could well say: "Here walks the ancient cloak, the old disguise, perhaps, of some Roundhead or Cavalier, of some cowled monk or holy nun, of some modern gentleman who has indulged in butchery or has himself been murdered – with new weapons but with the same old passions and hate behind him."(194)

I should like to link this idea with another that I take from the previously mentioned volume *Rapporto dalla Dimensione X*, which was compiled by Giorgio di Simone in order to collect the contents of the transcendental communications of another supposedly disincarnate spirit into a single anthology. In the passage I am about to quote Giorgio di Simone expresses himself in his own words, though what he says refers explicitly to the teachings of what he calls "Entity A" and, at the same time, is based on ideas that are quite widely held in spiritist circles. The disgregation of the physical body that takes place on death is followed by the disgregation of another reality that operates at a different vibration level. But let di Simone speak for himself: "Sooner or later the complex of the soul becomes disgregated, breaking up into its primary constitutive elements, which can subsequently be reorganized in a different way by another spirit and used for his own contacts and experiences, while the spirit that used them previously passes on to other levels, to higher experiences, with qualitatively superior instruments."(195) Although I personally completely disassociate myself from the type of reincarnationism that I see professed in the communications of "Entity A", as also in Giorgio di

Simone's writings in general, this does not in any way lessen the importance of the concept expressed in the passage I have just quoted, which seems to me to be very significant even from my own point of view and can be used also within the interpretative framework that I have here developed and proposed.

The entity "Myers" also makes it clear that, after abandoning his physical body (by means of what is known as death), a deceased subsequently also casts off something else. Indeed, "Myers" tells us that at a certain moment the etheric body is loosening, working out, withdrawing from the husk, until, at last, judgement is completed. At that point "the soul takes flight, casts the husk from him as a man throws an old cloak from off his shoulders".(196) This cloak or shell that the deceased is said to throw away is also referred to by "Myers" as "his skin . . . the tattered remnant that bound him to mortality".(197) In other words, what we are here concerned with is an "outer rind", an "After-image" that "has been flung away".(198) Just as the physical body does not seem to be the only vestment that a deceased abandons, one can say analogously that the "shell" to which "Myers" alludes is not the only etheric skin that the deceased succeeds in casting off after having abandoned his physical body.

"Myers" also alludes to the subsequent abandonment of a second shell, which he refers to as the "etheric body". According to "Myers", this casting off takes place at a more advanced state, at the end of a sojourn in a spiritual sphere that he calls the "Third Plane" or "Illusion-land" where the deceased, still dominated by the images and forms of their earthly life, ideoplastically create for themselves an environment that is very similar to the terrestrial one and they therefore vest themselves in corporeal images similar to the human body. As already noted, this situation bears a striking resemblance to what happens in our dream experiences.

At the end of this phase, too, it seems that the deceased cast off yet another shell. Indeed, "Myers" goes on to specify that at this stage they come to find themselves at a road junction, a parting of the ways. He says that there are those whom he calls "Soul-men", who "desire to return to earth or wish, at any rate, for some planetary existence wherein they may achieve some intellectual triumph, or wherein they may play a notable part in the strife of earthly or planetary life". These are the beings who "become reincarnate again" while "the majority of Soul-men slough their etheric body and put on a shape which is a degree finer".[199]

I do not know whether one has to accept in all its rigidity the distinction that "Myers" makes between the seven "planes" of this spiritual existence. But it is a fact that a condition of spiritual life very closely analogous to the one that "Myers" calls the "Third Plane" or the "Country of Illusions" recurs in the testimonies of spirits, who talk about something that could be defined as a "second death", following which the inhabitants of that plane are said to disappear without leaving any trace behind, presumably in order to ascend to a yet higher plane.

Let us now take a look at the testimony in this respect given by the entity "Doctor Scott" to his surviving wife, and reproduced in the book entitled *From Four who are Dead, Messages to C. A. Dawson Scott,* which is extensively quoted by Bozzano in his own book *La crisi della morte.*

When asked whether the people he had known on earth were to be found together with him in the spiritual environment in which he was then living, Doctor Scott replied that many of them had left for a – to him – unknown destination, though he subsequently added that this departure could be defined as a kind of second death that did not involve anything painful at all.[200]

We have already seen that the reincarnationism of many deceased, just like that of many men still living on this earth, is to be considered as a mere opinion. But there is a very important difference between the two cases, indeed, an essential one. Opinions expressed here on earth are ways of interpreting the realities around us and only very rarely can they assume the form of hallucinations in the proper sense of the term, while the material concreteness of the de facto realities remains what it is. On the plane of existence that we call "the beyond", on the other hand, every reality seems to be psychic. Where everything is psyche, thought is not limited to considering something that is objective and therefore remains distinct from it: if the whole of reality is psychic, thought will be *creating* reality at the very moment when it is thinking.

Opinions and beliefs therefore take shape and immediately assume the most tangible form. Even though it is quite possible that some more objective point of reference may remain here or there, the basic situation – for what it is worth – can surely be described as follows: having created a psychic reality in keeping with his own opinion, the subject remains surrounded by it as if it were a mental fog, which will become all the thicker when the opinion is a deeply rooted one. Although objective truth remains what it is, this mental fog could prevent the subject from seeing it or, at least, could strongly condition his vision.

One can therefore understand quite readily that a deceased who believes in reincarnation and aspires to becoming reincarnated will – by means of these mechanisms – receive an extremely vivid impression of actually being reincarnated (and here, once again, it does not matter whether this impression does or does not correspond to an objective reality: the impression will still be vivid, as dramatically vivid as certain illusions can be when they are perfect). Equally vivid could be the experience of other deceased in the same spiritual environment (and again it does not matter whether the experience is "real" or otherwise) who "see" (I advisedly write the verb in inverted commas) the given subject "reincarnate himself": they have taken note of his desire to go back on earth; and it may well be that while he vividly feels that he is on the way to the womb of a woman where a new creature is being conceived, they go through an equally vivid experience and are convinced that they "see" their companion leave them for this particular destination. If thereafter it is reasonable to expect the "reincarnate" to fall into a state of unconsciousness for the nine months of the gestation period, it is equally reasonable to suppose that from this moment onwards the others will simply note that he has disappeared from their environment.

One may even think that a certain number of these spirits who disappear without leaving any trace behind them do pass through a subjective experience of the reincarnation type before they ascend to the next spiritual level if at this point they feel a strong desire, an aspiration, an intimate need for passing through this type of experience.

May I ask my readers to forgive me if I let my imagination roam a little, but this is surely necessary if one wants to formulate any kind of hypothesis. Let us therefore imagine a deceased who, desirous of reincarnating, convinced that he can and must do so and having chosen the environment, the family and the mother for his next "reincarnation", effectively takes an initiative to this end. The result could well be that, rather than becoming reincarnated in the proper sense of the term, as the central core of his personality, that is, he simply succeeds in piloting his astral shell to the chosen destination or, in any case, some element of his psyche that is peripheral rather than central. Let us assume that this is what our deceased would effectively achieve, albeit with the illusion of having reincarnated his personality *in toto,* of having realized a reincarnation in keeping with traditional reincarnationist ideas.

When making such an attempt to pilot his own reincarnation, our hypothetical deceased could even succeed in achieving, at least to some limited extent, possession of the personality of a living person. Let us recall in this connection that Muller attributes certain possession phenomena to what he calls "ignorant spirits", to spirits who are unaware of their real condition.

We could therefore consider phenomenologies of the possession type to comprise also cases of deceased who believe they have become reincarnated (in a certain manner, *in toto* that is), whereas in actual fact they have done no more than pilot the limited reincarnation of a peripheral element of their psychism.

An illusion of this kind could come to an end when the deceased enters a phase of drowsiness, possibly followed by one of deep sleep, during which he casts off his astral shell, leaving it exactly where it finds itself at that moment, namely adhering to or incorporated in the new living individual that we could define as the "reincarnation" of the deceased, though only in a very loose and broad sense of the term.

The subjective experience of a deceased who strongly desires to reincarnate and makes an attempt to pilot his reincarnation would therefore have to be considered as a partly illusory experience, because what effectively becomes reincarnated is not *himself* but only *something of himself.* Nevertheless, between this "himself" and this "something of himself" there also exists an intimate participation and a kind of participative identity: in this sense and within these limits, therefore, one may attribute to the experience under consideration also an aspect of *non-illusoriness,* of objective reality.

Inasmuch as he identifies himself with the fragment of his personality that is about to become effectively reincarnated, the deceased in question would reasonably expect to fall into a kind of sleep, which could either be wholly unconscious or, alternately, populated with dreams: with dreams of a particular kind and having a very particular function.

At this point it may be helpful to make a brief excursus to establish a parallel with another kind of sleep that, as certain recurring communications suggest, comes to envelop some deceased immediately after their demise.

The tenth of the thirty-six cases examined by Bozzano in *La crisi della morte* contains a testimony, according to which many of the deceased fall asleep as soon as they have become disincarnate. This is said to happen to deceased who thought death to be equivalent to annihilation, "so that the period of restoring sleep at first seemingly confirms their convictions in this connection. These deceased need no explanation or assistance until the end of their period of rest, which sometimes can be very lengthy, especially when their convictions regarding the non-existence of the soul were very deeply rooted".[201]

Basing himself on a comparative analysis of a large number of cases, Bozzano feels himself to be in a position to say in this connection that "according to information provided by deceased, the spirits of disincarnates who right up to their death remained convinced of final annihilation normally fall into a deep sleep as soon as they become immersed in the spiritual world and then remain in this state for years and even decades; this is due to the circumstance that the inveterate convictions in this sense often go hand in hand with ways of life that are in keeping with their convictions: that is to say, they live without aiming at anything other than accumulating money by every possible means, desirous of enjoying life in an egoistic and animal-like manner without even the shadow of an ideal to nobilitate them, be it social, moral, scientific or artistic, and altruistic behaviour is unknown to them; in this way they imitate the ancient Romans, who in their period of decadence engaged in nefarious orgies and sang in chorus: 'Let's get drunk with wine and love, for life is short and everything ends with death'."[202]

This somewhat picturesque description gives us quite a good idea of the category of deceased who are involved here. But let us not forget that as far as certain things and certain values are concerned, there are also many unbelievers who are so only in a doctrinal or theoretical sense and in actual existential terms often behave far more like believers than many professed believers: Bozzano's passage, clearly, does not refer to men of this type.

Having mentioned the possibility of such a sleep experience (possibly populated by particular dreams), I think it would be useful to try to establish a certain parallel by comparing the sleep into which fall the deceased who are convinced that they are about to reincarnate with the sleep that for a certain period of time envelops the newly deceased who, while still "alive", were profoundly and vitally convinced that the soul must die at the same time as the body. Let us bear in mind, however, that there would seem to be the following difference between the two situations: those who are convinced that they die entirely upon the death of their physical body identify themselves (i.e. the whole of their personality) with that body, while convinced reincarnationists identify themselves (again in the sense of their entire personality) with the astral shell that would seemingly be the only reality that effectively becomes reincarnated.

Let us therefore draw up a kind of table to list the differences between the two attitudes point by point. To this end we shall simplify matters by calling our two subjects (of which the first is convinced that he dies *wholly* with his body, while the second believes that he will become *totally* reincarnated) respectively A and B.

We can now establish our point-by-point parallelism by first noting a particular aspect of the behaviour or attitude of A and comparing it with the corresponding attitude or behaviour of B, stating the latter in parentheses in each case.

1) A is convinced that he *dies totally* on the occasion of the death of his body (B is convinced that the core of his personality *becomes totally reincarnated*)

2) A *identifies himself with his body* and the fate of that body (B, even though he does not realize it, *identifies himself* to all intents and purposes *with his astral shell* and the fate of that shell, which effectively becomes reincarnated)

3) A falls asleep, i.e. falls into a kind of long *sleep* that may also be associated with *dreams* (B does something very similar)

4) When he eventually awakes from this sleep, A comes to acquire a clear consciousness of his real condition, i.e. he becomes fully aware of the fact that his soul, *the true nucleus of his disincarnate personality, has really survived* the death of his physical body (analogously, B acquires ever clearer awareness of the fact that *what has become reincarnated is not the core of his personality but only one of its peripheral elements,* a mere psychic shell that he has abandoned in much the same way as it had previously abandoned the physical body)

5) On *awaking*, A finds himself not only fully aware of his effective condition as a spirit who has survived in the beyond, but is also fully

reconciled with this condition (analogously, B finds himself far more reconciled with his condition as a deceased who is not destined to become reincarnated).

One element that stands out as much in one case as it does in the other is a certain attachment to the earth, a feeling that somehow has to be slept off before the deceased can become *fully* adapted to the conditions of life in the spiritual world. This sleep could well be animated by some special dreams, by some particular oneiric or quasi-oneiric experiences: if this is so, it would have the very specific function of acting as an outlet, a digestion period as it were, designed to usher in a state of satiety and thus to mark the full consummation of that experience and, at the same time, its surmounting.

As regards these "sleep" phases, "Myers" has let it be known that "between each plane there is this lapse into apparent oblivion, a stilling of all processes, a great calm".[203] Moreover, testimonies from beyond seem to agree to a very striking extent as regards this period of sleep or drowsiness that either coincides with demise or follows hard upon it, a case in point being the testimonies reproduced in Bozzano's *La crisi della morte.*[204]

This sleep would thus have the function of promoting detachment: detachment from the physical body, subsequent detachment from other bodies or subtler shells, liberation from any and all forms of attachment. We may therefore regard this sleep as performing a therapeutic or liberatory function by acting in a direction diametrically opposed to that of repression of the instincts and their consequent "removal". The deceased gradually free themselves from these attachments by giving "free vent" to them, "digesting" them to the best possible extent: if this is the function of dream-populated sleep, the deep sleep that follows it or alternates with it would have the equally necessary and, indeed, complementary function of acting as a period of distension and calm.

In fact, there is a great deal of attachment to things of the earth that has to be "digested". Some hints in this connection are provided by the previously mentioned *Letters from a Living Dead Man,* where "Judge Hatch" speaks, among others, of a new friendship he has made in the other world, namely the boy Lionel, whom we already had occasion to note in a previous quotation: "He is all interest in regard to certain things I have told him about the earth – especially aeroplanes, which were not yet very practicable when he came out. *He wants to go back* and fly in an aeroplane. I tell him that he can fly here without one, but that does not seem to be the same thing to him. He wants to get his fingers on machinery."[205] Just before this the late judge had briefly mentioned "instances where the soul goes back very soon, with little rest", which he said happened in the case of *"a soul with great curiosity and strong desires"*.[206]

Elsewhere in the same book there is a dramatically vivid passage to tell us what happens in these cases or, more exactly, what subjective experiences can be lived by the deceased in such a situation: "Suddenly the call of matter, the eager, terrible call of blood and warmth, of activity raised to the *n*th power, catches the half-awakened soul on the ethereal side of matter" and thus "he has again entered the world of material formation. He is sunk and hidden in the flesh of earth. He awaits birth".[207]

It would indeed seem that among the souls who have passed over there is a good number who feel this longing, this great desire to reincarnate, reincarnation being seemingly the means of placating this desire, this psychologic need. In some way, therefore, these deceased satisfy this need of theirs in a manner analogous to a hungry person who, unable to eat for one reason or another, can yet provide a certain satisfaction for the associated psychologic need by dreaming that he is feasting to his heart's content at a magnificent banquet.

That certain attachments can be digested and overcome by means of a psychologic outlet of this type, obtainable if necessary by passing through a hallucinatory and even obsessive experience, would also seem to be suggested by something said by "Myers" in a somewhat different context, though it can readily be integrated into our present subject matter and approach, completing it as it were and throwing light on another possible dimension. Given the complexity and delicacy of the problem under consideration, however, it will be best to let "Myers" explain it in his own words, albeit at some length: "Now, I would give you one more illustration. Let us take for example a man, or if you prefer a woman, who has led an immoral life on earth. Here I may borrow a saying of the angel who appeared to John: 'He that is filthy let him be filthy still.' (Rev. 22,11). The man who comes into this life with a sex history of a reprehensible kind finds, when he enters the Kingdom of the Mind, that as his mental perceptions are sharpened so his predominant earth-desire is intensified, his mental power being far more considerable. He can, at will, summon to himself those who will gratify this overdeveloped side of his nature. Others of his kind gravitate toward him. And for a time these beings live in a sex paradise. But bear in mind that it is created by their mental 'make-up', by their memories and their imagination. They yearn still for gross sensations, not for that finer life, which is the spirit of sexual love, that perfect comradeship without the gratification of the grosser feelings.

"They obtain it in abundance, and there follows a horrible satiety. They come to loathe what they can obtain in excess and with ease; and then they find it extraordinarily difficult to escape from those who share their pleasures with them.

"A murderer comes into the category of such men. It is a sudden perverted desire, a lust for cruelty which leads in many cases to murder.

"The last state in Illusion-land might be termed the purgatorial state. Obviously, it is extremely painful to realise the misery of satiety, to come to the end of the desired pleasure. There is one greater misfortune than the non-realisation of the heart's desire and that is its realisation. For human beings are so constituted that they are almost invariably seeking a false dream, a will-o'-the-wisp, and no permanent content can be obtained from its fulfilment."(208)

The long passage I have just quoted gives us a very good and vivid idea of how the total consummation of earthly desires and attachments can be pursued and obtained in the spiritual world, i.e. after death, by means of a kind of experience that can be defined at least partly, at least to some extent, as oneiric and hallucinatory. What "Myers" tells us clearly brings out the function that these experiences can perform in providing an outlet and thus promoting surfeit, a function that could well be described as cathartic, as leading – albeit indirectly – to purification.

In the last resort, therefore, these oneiric or hallucinatory experiences, these "dreams" (which may possibly alternate with periods of deeper and unconscious sleep), would seem to serve the purpose of providing an outlet for all the residues of earthly attachments, the residues of desires, ambitions, passions, etc., thus enabling the subject to break free of them once and for all. More particularly, in the case of subjects convinced that they die totally with their physical body, this oneiric and hallucinatory experience, together with the phases of deeper sleep that accompany it, would seem to have the function of helping them to overcome not only this conviction of theirs, but also the whole of their materialistic *forma mentis,* as well as the mental habits bound up therewith. Again, in the case of subjects convinced of a total reincarnation involving the central core of their personality, an analogous phase of oneiric or hallucinatory experiences, followed or broken by phases of complete unconsciousness, would evidently have the function of helping them to fully overcome their "reincarnationitis", as well as all the earthly attachments that may sustain it.

In a manner altogether analogous to what is thought to happen in the course of these variegated experiences of the oneiric and/or hallucinatory type, a "reincarnative" experience conceived in this manner would also have to be followed by a definitive awakening. Upon so "awaking", a subject – let me repeat this – who was convinced that he had reincarnated as a person, would find himself substantially reconciled to his condition as a deceased not destined to become reincarnated *in toto;* moreover, having by that time overcome the reincarnation sickness that derived from his many earthly attachments, he would presumably come to find himself in a very different spiritual environment, in different company as it were: for the law of affinity would ensure that the new and no longer reincarnationist convictions of our subject would now find their counterpart in an environment in which reincarnation (in the sense that has here been subjected to criticism) is rejected by common conviction. Our subject would therefore be obliged to recognize the partly "true" and partly "false" but always illusory character of his own reincarnative experience.

At this point we may ask ourselves whether a deceased who has gone through this process would be able to communicate his new insights to his former reincarnationist companions. I believe that this would be very difficult, because it seems likely that each of his old companions will in the meantime have followed a road of his own, so that at this stage he will be reachable only as an individual, but not together with all the others.

Indeed, a comparative analysis of the "communications" has given me the impression that if there exists a similar beyond, it must be a spiritual world that is not only extensively subdivided, a world with "many rooms" as it were, but also extremely fluid and subject to continuous change. In other words, I derive a clear impression that each individual spiritual environment is destined to dissolve after a relatively short period of time, or at least to become radically modified, as the spirits that formed part of it evolve and transfer to other levels, an outflow compensated by the continuous influx of new spirits, each of whom capable of introducing even the most radical transformations by virtue of his creative mental powers.

In this connection we may draw some support and comfort from the testimony of the entity "Raymond", said to be the son (a war victim) of Sir Oliver Lodge, a well-known metapsychist. Here is what "Raymond" told him: "Father, we're obliged to create conditions, and what you might call *things, on our plane*. They've only got *a temporary life*."[209]

All appearances suggest that associative life in the beyond is of a wholly spontaneous nature: though regulated in its essentials by a hierarchy of spirits that becomes constituted in a wholly natural manner on the basis of the level attained by each one, it is yet devoid of the characteristic that in our earthly world underlie what we call social "organization"; there is no stability of juridical relations, no real permanence in the various environments or of the environments themselves, just as there are no permanent communities or anything that could lead one to think of our agencies, cities or villages with their stable government organs, their executives, their secretariats, their archives and record offices, their protocol, their stamps, etc., in short, none of the things that earthly societies need by very virtue of their material consistence and stability, their decidedly belonging to a world that is necessarily dominated by concepts and numbers, by science, technology, positive law and a political, economic and social organization that is becoming ever more capillary and sophisticated.

What has been briefly discussed here makes it abundantly clear that in the spiritual world it is impossible – or, at least, for the moment extremely difficult – to have a kind of universal scientific congress to enable the spirits to reach agreement once and for all as to how things effectively stand in relation to reincarnation (or otherwise) and to solve many other problems of various kinds.

Moreover, stable and durable relations between non-kindred and dissentient souls would seem to be made particularly difficult by the fact that, in a dimension where the psyche is all, where thought is all, the very conflicts of opinion regarding the existential realities would automatically generate two or more dissimilar modes of *existing:* in a sphere where like attracts like, and attracts it *physically* I would say, just as it physically repels the unlike, those who hold identical or similar view about fundamental matters would end up by being physically attracted to each other and, consequently, existing in physical proximity either in the same environment or in readily communicating environments, while those who are far removed from each other in their ways of thinking would repel each other and would therefore end up by existing at great physical distances from each other, so that they would also experience concrete difficulty in communicating and, even more so, establishing regular relations and contacts with each other.

In a situation like the one I have described on the basis of the ideas and impressions that I have been able to gain of the other world, ideas that are as yet admittedly rather vague, one can readily understand that each deceased, even more so than people living on earth, can stick to his own opinions, all the more so as his opinions no longer have to take account of the corrective of "science", so that he will be almost completely unbridled and he can therefore create ideoplastic confirmation of his views as he pleases.

It remains for us to examine the problem of the other spirits who believe in reincarnation and have been left behind in a given etheric environment after our subject has gone away to become reincarnated. We may imagine that our deceased, desirous of becoming reincarnated, will have announced his intentions, his imminent departure, and that, illuding himself as to the possibility of realizing this reincarnation in the manner traditionally believed, he will have projected himself in the direction of the chosen (or, in any case, available) matrix. One may reasonably suppose that his companions will have seen him disappear. He has effectively passed through what is often called a "second death".

Better still, one might say that our would-be reincarnate is realizing or achieving his "second death" via the complex itinerary of a pseudo-reincarnation: that is to say, via a reincarnation that we can consider such only in an extremely elastic and, on the whole, improper sense, as we have already shown rather exhaustively.

There are some who consider this "second death" as a going back to earth for another incarnation, just as there are others who consider it purely and simply as an elevation to a subtler sphere of spiritual life after having abandoned yet another astral shell, an outer wrapping that would serve no useful purpose at the new level or, rather, would even constitute an impediment there. However one wants to interpret this second death, what effectively happens is that our subject disappears from view, so that his "companions" no longer see him about.

What, then, could be the convictions of those who were his companions in the given spiritual environment, the spirits he has left behind there? What could be their attitude? I can imagine that, having seen him disappear (and disappear completely), his former fellow reincarnationists will remain convinced that he has effectively gone to reincarnate on earth (and that he has become reincarnated in a total manner, with the very core of his personality, as required by traditional reincarnation doctrine), even though – for reasons that we have already examined – this is not exactly what has happened.

Over and above this, I can also imagine that among the spirits we have described as his fellow reincarnationists there will be some who have taken the commitment not only of helping the presumed reincarnation of our aspiring returnee in the womb of the woman who should become his new mother, but also of assisting the newborn baby (the presumed reincarnate, that is) in his new earthly existence. These tutelary spirits or guardian angels or spirit guides (whatever one may wish to call them) will absolve this function in accordance with the commitment they have assumed and in the conviction that those they assist on earth are the full and total reincarnation of the deceased they had already taken under their wings at the time when, together with them, they found themselves in the given spiritual environment and were convinced that they had to reincarnate at the earliest possible moment.

This does not in any way alter the fact that these newly conceived individuals can, at the very most, be reincarnations of mere astral shells of the deceased concerned. If this is true, the affection of these guardian angels would be showered on to something that is no more than the residue of the personality of these deceased, and not their personality *in toto*, in the proper sense of the term that is. On the other hand, it would seem that what interests them is not the personality of their protegé with all its individual characteristics: indeed, these spirits are well prepared to detach themselves from a personality conceived in this manner, in which their ideology (as also their selfsame sensitivity) sees nothing other than a threadbare garment to be discarded and destined to disintegrate just like the physical body. What really interests them is not the person of Tom, say, but rather Tom as an "individual".

Reduced to an individual, Tom seems so completely stripped of every personal note that he could easily be mistaken for the individual to be found under the personality of Dick, or of Harry for that matter, and nobody would note the difference if it were not for the fact that to distinguish one individuality from another there is the different fruit of that person's actions, the different karma. Not even I have ever called into doubt that the psychic residues of a deceased that become reincarnated bring with them the fruit of the actions that the given deceased has performed during the course of his earthly existence.

The tutelar spirits of this deceased are not interested in what happens to his personality, they are concerned with what happens to the fruit of his actions. And they can readily see where this karma is going to reincarnate. They know that it is going to reincarnate in the newly-born Dick, and that is sufficient for them. Following the new existence of Dick, they can really see what developments will be undergone by Tom's karma sown in the personality of Dick, for Dick receives this karma like more or less fertile virgin land, thus making possible all kinds of new syntheses. In these new syntheses, as already in the old ones that occurred during the previous existence of Tom, the personality element will still count for little or nothing in the eyes of certain reincarnationists: wrongly so, to my mind at least, but this is of no importance to them. What they are concerned with is to follow the karma in its successive passages, and they are content if they can do so.

At this point we may also ask ourselves whether in some cases, an undefined number of cases let us say, it would not be possible for the personality to become reincarnated with all its essential nucleus: that is to say, whether Tom could not reincarnate in the new human being Dick specifically as Tom and not as the mere psychic residue of Tom (though laden with the fruit of his actions).

I think that to configure such a hypothesis, to make it more concrete, one would have to imagine a kind of *possession,* a possession *sui generis,* with certain very particular characteristics that I will not try to define. Firstly, it is obvious that this would not be a temporary possession of a medium, but *a permanent or ongoing possession.* Tom's disincarnate personality would take possession of the organism of the child Dick at a very early stage that could even precede birth itself. The conditioning to which Tom's possessing personality would become subject in an as yet unevolved receiving personality would substantially limit the awareness that Tom has of himself, so much so that he could even feel himself to be Dick in all things: Dick who is in the early stages of his existence and remembers nothing about the fact that he has already lived as Tom.

Memories of this kind could come to the fore at a later state, either as the result of hypnotic regression or even spontaneously so. Having assumed a possession that goes back to the early years of Dick's life, or to birth or even to the period of prenatal existence in his mother's womb, one can equally assume that this possession will come to an end only on the occasion of the physical death of the possessed personality. But we may well ask whether this personality, which by convention we call the personality of Dick, ought not to be considered as belonging to Dick himself. In other words, what happens to Dick?

In cases in which an incarnate personality is possessed by a disincarnate personality, the latter occupies the former to a certain extent, while the possessed subject may either remain conscious (when the possession is *partial,* as it were) or sink into unconsciousness (as in cases where the medium is *totally* possessed, either temporarily or for a long period of time). In the case here considered we have postulated total and prolonged possession of Dick's personality by the personality of Tom: so prolonged as to extend over a period of time of great length, beginning possibly at the very birth of Dick (or even before) and brought to an end only by Dick's physical death. Considering this case, the subject Dick, together with what constitutes the conscious nucleus of his personality, would remain latent, that is to say, would remain in the state of an unrepressed potential. This means that he could express himself, blossom forth and acquire consciousness of himself (in short: realize himself as a true subject) only at some time after his physical death: that is to say, at a moment when his personality (or, rather, what remains of it at the purely psychic level) at long last becomes liberated from the long occupation by somebody else's personality.

The effective result, however, would simply be this: in order to concede himself the luxury of living two earthly lives, Tom would to all intents and purposes deprive Dick of the right to live his own. Of course, it is quite true that Dick could subsequently right the score at the expense of some other personality about to be born. But this would be rather like playing musical chairs and create a situation not very different from what happens in barracks when a recruit finds that somebody has stolen his helmet, water-bottle, mess tin or any other item of his personal issue: if these articles are not numbered or identified by some other mark, the problem is quickly and effectively solved: the victim simply helps himself to the issue of a companion, who then takes that of a third, and so on.

However, one could also postulate a somewhat different situation, namely that Tom reincarnates *in toto* in the mere mould of a new incarnate personality in which no subjectivity *in se* has yet become constituted; and in which no subjectivity *in se* could ever become constituted by virtue of the fact that this function, right from the very beginning, is being absolved by Tom's own personality. Inserting itself into the new personality germ coming into existence in the mother's womb, becoming grafted on to it as it were, Tom's pre-existing personality, by very virtue of the fact that there is no Dick as a personality, would thus assume the new personality, merging it with itself to the point of constituting a single and no longer separable whole.

This, admittedly, is a hypothesis that can always be formulated, though it is extremely difficult to support and convalidate it with facts; indeed, the phenomena that are normally adduced in support of reincarnation seem to suggest not the absorption of the personality of the possessed in that of the possessor, but rather the very opposite. That Dick's incarnate personality which appears before our eyes should contain nothing of an *autonomous* subjectivity of Dick cannot therefore be considered as anything other than a purely abstract hypothesis, something that is wholly devoid of any element of confirmation in concrete phenomenology.

The hard facts tell us that we are faced with Dick, the present living subject, who in a certain phase may even lose the sense of his identity, his sense of being Dick, but sooner or later will regain it and, what is more, will normally regain it reinforced, stronger than it was before.

We have indeed dwelt at length on this particular aspect, backing it up with every possible fact and argument. Nevertheless, one can always say or claim that this Dick who seems to absorb so well the impact of another personality is nothing other than Tom, who has become so totally and fully reincarnated in a Dick that was such only in embryo and never became realized as a personality *in se*: so that, notwithstanding the loss of memory and the change of body and name, we were really always concerned with Tom.

As we have already said, such a hypothesis can always be formulated: but it is formulated in terms that make it quite impossible either to verify it or to demonstrate its falsity. As long as one remains on such a plane wholly inaccessible to experience, one can clearly say anything one likes, without any limits at all; equally clearly, however, such hypotheses remain completely abstract and arbitrary.

CHAPTER VII

Conclusions in the Light of Biblical, Christian and Humanist Traditions

As my readers can see, the very title of this last chapter already makes it clear that the final considerations I propose to make, the conclusions, will be couched in biblical, Christian and humanist terms. Let me say right away, however, that our problem here is not by any means to establish whether the Jews of antiquity and the early Christians were reincarnationists and, if so, to what extent; nor are we concerned with deciding whether or to what extent certain texts of the Bible or the Church Fathers lend themselves to a reincarnationist interpretation. Quite apart from any possible and always highly opinionable reincarnationist interpretation of some passage in the Bible or of some other text of early Christian traditions, I am primarily concerned with grasping and highlighting what seems to be the profound significance of the biblical and Christian tradition and to state it in a manner that can be accepted, lived and believed in by men of our own times.

What, first of all, shall we say about the claimed reincarnationism of the Jews and Christians in ancient times? I have no difficulty in accepting that reincarnationist ideas (taken, for example, from Hellenism) may have exercised some influence on the mentality and doctrine of Jews and Christians, especially some individuals or groups (and, above all, as history shows us, various schools and sects); but the reincarnationist interpretations of certain biblical passages that one so often hears are, taken on the whole, far-fetched and artificial, literally dragged in by the hair: this is admitted even by David Christie-Murray, to name but one, who reviews various biblical passages in the general context of a book he wrote to examine the reincarnationist beliefs and testimonies of all times and ages from his own particular viewpoint, which is that of a convinced reincarnationist.[210]

As regards this aspect, I shall therefore refer my readers to the well-balanced judgments of Christie-Murray (which thoroughly redimension the "hermeneutics fiction" of a multitude of other authors who seem to lie perennially in wait, ready to see reincarnation everywhere with a petulance close to obsession) and dedicate this last chapter to a series of more personal reflections. I shall limit myself to some observations, to a meditation in more markedly existential terms, based on the results attained in the course of this study, which had as its essential objective not reincarnation as such, as a doctrine, but rather the facts, the concrete phenomena suggestive of reincarnation.

I am well conscious of the gaps to be found in this volume even as regards the phenomena themselves. More than anything else, however, the booklet was intended as an essay, albeit a long one, without in any way claiming to constitute a complete treatment: it set out to do no more than offer some food for thought (and, as far as possible, also some data and references) for a clearly circumscribed discussion.

The kind of reincarnationism today so fashionable in the Western countries sees successive incarnations not so much as a succession of misfortunes or a series of possibilities that are offered to a soul to expiate its sins, but rather as a renewed possibility of gathering experiences. The experiences with which we are here concerned are of a certain type that can be had only in an earthly environment, that is to say, in a dimension of the densest materiality, in a dimension of objectivity.

Let us for a moment consider the markedly subjective, and I would even say transient and ephemeral, character that would seem to be associated with the experiences of a disincarnate subject in a purely psychic sphere of existence: this consideration by itself is quite sufficient to give us a good idea of just how salutary an occasional immersion in objectivity could be for a disincarnate spirit.

Even art stands in need of a dimension of materiality (the forms, the colours, the sounds, the words, etc.): it is precisely by taking matter as matter that art realizes itself as art at the very moment when, overcoming the resistance of matter, it transfigures it into spirit or, if you prefer, spiritualizes it. Art is therefore both spirit and matter, it has a material dimension that cannot be eliminated. As far as objectivity is concerned, matter is also the dimension of science, just as it is the dimension of any technological or organizational moment that humanism must pass through in order to realize itself.

A material moment cannot be eliminated from any instance of the spirit desirous of becoming transformed into deed by overcoming a resistance, employing a means, reducing a multiplicity to unity. It is not by chance that some philosophers have defined matter as the principle of individuation. It could also be defined as the principle of determination, of objectivity, and of concreteness. Without a material pole of some kind or other spirituality would dissolve into pure indifferentiation.

Without a material pole, no matter of what kind, spiritual life could be conceived only as a pure state of undifferentiated consciousness and could never be conceived as creation of a multiplicity, as an act of knowledge and love that has such a multiplicity as its object. Spirituality would still be possible as pure contemplation (or self-contemplation) of the resulting emptiness (in keeping with trends that have historically prevailed in certain oriental environments, especially Hinduist and Buddhist), but it would no longer be possible to have a creative humanist spirituality of the Western type, a spirituality that passes also through the love of the other inasmuch as he is "other" and is expressed also in art, in science, in technology, in organization.

The material or corporeal moment is so essential to a spirituality conceived in this manner that this spirituality cannot be truly and totally realized without passing also through matter and without returning to matter once it has become detached therefrom. Returning to matter means taking it in order to spiritualize it, but without thereby abolishing it as matter. It is not without significance that Christian-biblical eschatology speaks of the resurrection of the dead, of their recovering the material or corporeal dimension in the full sense of the term, even though in this connection there is mention of "a new heaven and a new earth" and of a corporeity transformed by the spirit in such a manner as to enable it to become a vehicle of the loftiest and most perfect spirituality.

If we place ourselves in this perspective, albeit accepting it only as a working hypothesis, we can readily understand how important it may be for a deceased to be able to return from time to time to immerse himself in the material dimension and even in the densest material vibration.

If the deceased can look forward to a resurrection understood as full and definitive recovery of the material-corporeal dimension (be it even a perfectly spiritualized corporeity, but not for that reason, let me say so again, any the less corporeal), these periodic returns to earth could have the function of preparing for this eschatological event, to prefigure it, to anticipate it to some extent. It seems to me that this idea expresses the truly valid core of the reincarnative instance, because here reincarnation is no longer seen as something that, when all is said and done, is desired as the result of an as yet unattained spiritual maturity, but rather as a legitimate need for returning and making the experiences necessary to promote further maturation.

As we have already said, optimal realization would consist of the full recovery of a material and corporeal condition that would also be the vehicle of the loftiest spirituality. If this seems to be the supreme objective to be pursued even in the disincarnate condition, we immediately come face to face with a new problem, for we now have to ask ourselves how the disincarnate can anticipate or prepare themselves, albeit in a limited and imperfect manner, for this recovery of the earthly dimension that they expect some day to be realized in perfect form on the occasion of resurrection.

One of the essential (though limited) ways in which the deceased can return to participate in earthly life would consist of a whole series of active interventions. When we look at the primitive and archaic religions, we find that, as a general rule, they are characterized by an attitude of concern towards the newly dead, whose intervention in the world of the living can become infestive in nature by very virtue of the fact that the deceased has not yet fully passed over, has not yet been wholly acquired to his new dimension. Something that can prove particularly troublesome (and also strongly negative) is the persisting presence of souls that, although they have abandoned the physical body, have in many ways remained attached to our world (*earthbound* according to a well known expression) and dominated by passions and excessive concern that cause them to act at our level in a manner that, for the most part, we don't like at all.

In earlier chapters we have already tried to characterize the condition of these souls, basing ourselves on the available phenomenology and the more significant and coherent testimonies. Seen in this light, what we have said here goes a long way toward explaining the significance that normally attaches to the funeral rites customary among primitive peoples: as Alfonso Di Nola puts it, "the ritual structures tend to free the deceased from negative and risky charges and, via the mechanism of placation, make him useful to the group . . . In this sense, therefore, the deceased is transformed into a forebear, that is to say, into somebody who has lived earlier and now continues to live and to manifest himself actively and more powerfully in a useful and beneficial direction".[211]

More particularly, the history of Orthodox and Catholic Christianity is literally crowded with episodes that suggest a continuous and beneficial intervention of "saints" after their bodily death. This widespread and continuous interest, this loving, beneficial and powerful participation in the life of men incarnate on this earth, finds its loftiest expression in some words pronounced by Saint Theresa of Lisieux not very long before she died at a very young age: "I am not looking forward to a feast of rest in Heaven. That is not what attracts me. What attracts me is love: to love, to be loved, and to come back to earth to cause God to be loved, to help the missionaries, the priests, the whole of the Church: I want to spend my Heaven by doing good on earth."[212]

A very important idea seems to emerge and to take shape from all this: the return to earth of those who have passed over can represent something negative as long as the deceased remain earthbound, attached to their former life; once they become fully acquired to their new and ultraterrestrial dimension, that is to say, when they have truly passed over, their return to earth assumes a very concrete and positive sense. Once the deceased can really be considered such, it can never be harmful to his status as a deceased to return to earth every now and again to do some good work, to return to earth from time to time to help the incarnate to realize themselves fully at every level, i.e. not on in a mystico-religious sense but also in the humanist earthly sense, because the perfection to which man tends is but a single and integrated whole.

Apart from action, another essential manner in which the deceased can come back to participate in earthly life is represented by knowledge. That the deceased, *as such*, continue (or at least can continue) to take an interest in what happens to the people they have left behind on this earth (as also to their own family or tribe or people, their own religious community or church) is a fact that is brought out by the almost chorus-like agreement of a truly large number of "communications"; what is more, it is also something that is clearly implicit in the series of active interventions that we have already mentioned: where there is an active intervention or participation, there must also be a motive of interest.

This interest in the things of the world and the troubles of living men can also extend to the past. While we who are still incarnate can study the past by going to the places where its traces still remain, by visiting its monuments and examining documents, all the time integrating these direct contacts with historical reading, it seems that the deceased can immerse themselves in even more vivid forms of knowledge, a good example of which is provided by a "communication" in Ernesto Bozzano's *La crisi della morte*, from which I have already quoted on several occasions. Here are the words used by a presumed entity in sneaking to his incarnate interlocutor: "A little while before I spoke to you I was at a ruined town in North Africa. I looked backward from the ruin through the phases of its existence."[213]

This is a form of knowledge that closely recalls, what at our own level, especially in parapsychology, is known as "psychometry" or "clairvoyance in the past". But here, still in the words of the deceased making the communication, are the stages through which this knowledge (obtained, as it were, by "identifying" oneself with the subject) is deepened by "seeing" events that gradually become more remote in time: "A decaying town, a populous town, a village, big wells and trees, a resting place for the nomad. One or two settled families. The first who brought there his wife and children. I saw back to the far-off day before man came, then before the great beasts came, when crawling water covered the soft ground and the air was thick mist, and farther still into the dimness of cooling fires wherein was no life."[214]

The long passage I have just quoted gives us quite a detailed and concrete idea of the *modus operandi* of this intuitive knowledge, in which the subject immerses himself in things as if he wanted to know them from within and ends up by reliving them in a most intensely dramatic manner; this is something that happens in many of the phenomena of psychometry, a classic case in point being provided by the experiments conducted by Dr. Gustav Pagenstecher with the help of the sensitive medium Maria Reyes de Zierold.[215]

Another problem that arises here is the one explained by yet another passage from Bozzano's book I have just quoted: "In these excursions of ours into the abysses of the past we have to be extremely cautious before we locate in time the things we contemplate, for it is easy to mistake what was for what exists at present. In fact, the reality of the two representations seems identical, and is effectively so, because every representation of the past contemplated by us does really exist in time, preserved in the ether; since this is so, we have to reflect and compare before we can say whether we are concerned with something that was or something that is."[216]

Anyone familiar with clairvoyance experiments will immediately understand the substance of this concern, this appeal for caution in discernment. Since thought in the psychic environment is immediately creative, it seems to me that another reason for caution becomes imperative and it is this: one has to be careful not to confuse what is (or has been) in effective reality with what simply is (or has been) in our thoughts, in our personal and subjective interpretations of facts and events; in other words, we have to be careful not to confuse the Egypt that is (today) or was (in successive epochs of its history) with what is nothing other than *our* way of seeing Egypt, with all the things that various people think or have thought about Egypt. In fact, the cosmic reservoir of memories would seem to contain not only the recollections of the things that were, but also of the things that have been thought, especially things that have been thought with intense and dramatic vivacity: and it would seem that even these subjective recollections can be projected into the present, made to relive with the same vivacity as representations of facts.

In this connection readers should recall our earlier examination of presumed memories of previous incarnations, where we saw that a hypnotized subject can relive these "memories" in the first person and in a highly dramatic manner, even though they represent nothing other than an altogether subjective elaboration of his mind.

Somewhat in line with these psychic incursions into the past is another type of revisitation that, according to the entity "Myers", can be carried out in the other dimension. "Myers" tells us about it in a second book he wrote through the hand of the medium Geraldine Cummins and entitled *Beyond Human Personality*. This second book also contains a chapter dedicated to reincarnation, where the phenomenon is mentioned as something that happens far less frequently than is thought by the great majority of reincarnationists.[217] The author also mentions the possibility that a "young soul", on incarnating to commence its own earthly existence, may assume the karma transmitted to it by a soul that has passed over. This concept would not be considered "right" by a reincarnationist of the current type and it is not therefore surprising to see it criticized by Bozzano;

but there remains the fact that it provides a considerable degree of confirmation for the reincarnation concept I have tried to develop in these pages.

But let me now briefly illustrate the type of revisitation of an earthly existence that "Myers" puts forward as something he claims to be possible in his dimension. There are relations of affinity between souls, so that souls united by certain affinities come to form a "group". Within a given group, as "Myers" goes on to tell us, a soul can – as it were – revisit what was or is, or even will be, the "earthly voyage" of another. The affinity that unites the members of one and the same group does not by any means consist of the fact that these subjects are very similar and live in similar conditions; rather, they are found to be very different from each other, with equally different experiences of life, so that what binds them together seems rather to consist of the fact that their diversity makes these subjects complementary. They therefore form a group in order to complete each other, and it is also to complete each other that each of them revisits the experiences of earthly life of the others and lives them as if they were his own.

Here are some of the things that "Myers" has to say in this connection. "I have not, at any time, been a member of the yellow races, but there are souls in my Group who have known and lived that eastern life, and I may, and do, enter into every act and emotion in their past chronicles."[218] . . . "Through our communal existence I perceive and feel the drama in the earthly journey of a Buddhist priest, of an American merchant, of an Italian painter, and I am, if I assimilate the life thus lived, spared the living of it in the flesh."[219] . . . "It is not necessary for us to return to earth to gather into our granary this manifold variety of life and knowledge. We can reap, bind and bring much of it home by participating in the life of our group-soul. Many belong to it and these may spread themselves in their journeys over past, present and future."[220] As already mentioned, the term "journey" is here used to designate a single earthly existence.

"Myers" does not tell us a great deal about these groups or group souls; but, apart from noting the fact as such, what I am particularly anxious to underline here is the possibility for each one of us to gather the fruit of what others have done and experienced in the course of their earthly existence. Here we are already far removed from the logic, characteristic of a certain type of reincarnationism, according to which an individual must do everything by himself and gather the fruit of only his own experiences and that anything else would be "unjust", not "right". Here, indeed, we enter a very different logic, a logic that, when fully developed, proves to be the very logic that implicitly underlies ideas like the one that sees people form part of one and the same "mystic body": it is the logic expressed in the well known biblical image of the vine and the shoots that the Church was subsequently to develop into the article of faith that affirms the "communion of the saints".

To enter into the existences of others is like entering into an enlarged self, where one's own capacity of knowledge and perception, one's own capacity of willing, can grow to the utmost degree; it makes it possible to strengthen one's character enormously, to acquire an immense spiritual strength, just as it makes it possible to "gather the wisdom of the ages" while continuing to preserve one's own "identity" and "fundamental individuality" without having to pass through the continuous 'sturm und drang' of hundreds of years passed in the confinement of the crude physical body".[221]

If I have rightly understood him, it would seem that it is extremely important for "Myers" to preserve the sense of his identity and continuity, a sense that, obviously, receives a decisive contribution from the conservation of memories of the past. While "Myers" clearly expresses a very positive appreciation as regards preservation of one's sense of identity and continuity, it seems to me that he sees in a rather negative light the idea that one has to go back continuously to become confined within the crude physical materiality of one's body, although this would seem to be something perfectly normal in the eyes of most traditional reincarnationists. It is true that "Myers" continues to admit the reality of a reincarnation in line with these traditional schemes so current today, but at the same time he points in a direction that could well lead to the overcoming of these schemes and is, in any case, well in line with the concepts I have here developed and proposed.

The reincarnationism of ancient times saw these successive incarnations as a sad necessity, something that an individual was obliged to suffer as a result of his negative karma. Reincarnation was therefore understood as the negative consequence of past errors or, alternately, as the negative consequence of the continuance of a state of imperfection that men were admonished to leave behind them as quickly as possible in order to realize the ideal of never having to reincarnate again. The point of view that sees reincarnation as a positive fact and an instrument of progress, a means of "gaining experience", seems to me to be far more typical of a modern form of reincarnationism that differs from its older counterpart, the original reincarnationism of antiquity, about as much as night differs from day.

In the great thread of Indian spirituality that runs from the Upanishads to Buddhism, indeed, the world and matter are tendentially felt as something negative, so that reincarnation is viewed rather like a sentence or condemnation, that is to say, as a negative consequence that derives automatically from a manner of acting that was defined as negative. The reincarnationism of our own days, on the other hand, is in keeping with concepts that began to take shape during the nineteenth century and views reincarnation as something positive, seeing in it the possibility of gathering new experiences of incarnate life in this world; it welcomes this possibility with a certain enthusiasm, or so it would seem, not least because being able to live once more in this world seems to many people to be the only conceivable form of survival.

Indeed, there is nothing more "modern" than this desire for an indefinite extension of one's earthly and bodily existence (albeit in an ever new and different context). But at the same time it would be difficult to find something more in contrast with the spirit of the Upanishads, the spirit of Buddhism, the spirit of a certain type of Hinduist ascesis and even the spirit that pervades the existential philosophy of Plotinus, all of which see the world in a radically negative light and pursue salvation, self-realization through escape from the world.

Biblical spirituality does not escape the world, but sees the loftiest and ultimate goal of the process of cosmico-historical becoming in the completion or fulfilment of the creation. But this perfect world that creation pursues as its ultimate goal consists of "a new heaven and a new earth": it is a perfect world in which our present condition will be completely left behind, just as the corporeity to be assumed by the resurrected is a glorious and completely transfigured corporeity, a perfect vehicle of the loftiest spirituality.

In this perspective, undoubtedly, the deceased aspire to a corporeity, without which they feel they lack something that is truly essential to their full and complete realization. But the corporeity to which they aspire is far removed from being the corporeity of our present condition of men, with all its limits and shortcomings. The indefinite duration of so imperfect a condition, or the continuous return to this condition for an indefinite period of time, would be felt as something negative in the light of a spiritual perspective like that of the Bible, as something that cannot but constitute an obstacle to progress. Even "Myers", from whose "communications" we have taken the concepts we have just reviewed, does not seem to care very much for the idea of a reincarnation that on each occasion encloses man in a corporeity as imperfect as our present one and, what is more, making him lose all memory not only of what he has learnt before but even of his personal identity.

Although it is very dear to reincarnationists of a certain type, the idea that learning ever new things in successive phases of existence requires one to forget on each occasion everything one has learnt before seems truly absurd to our eyes, for the mere thought of such a labour as futile as that of Sisyphus cannot but clash with all our pedagogic concepts (themselves the result of a long toil), with a pedagogy that very rightly emphasizes the quite irreplaceable part that memory plays in the learning process. " . . . *Non fa scienza / senza lo ritenere, avere inteso,*" wrote Dante long ago (Understanding without remembering does not add up to science).[222]

The only memory that is meaningful for us, the only memory that can really be defined as such, is the concrete memory we have, the memory of which we make concrete use: such is the empiric memory of facts, events and realities we remember at this moment and which, basing ourselves on our fundamental memory (again as of this moment), we can translate into deed or action here and now, using rapid and straightforward consulting procedures. There is no such thing as an "essential memory" that eventually, faced with all the needs inherent in our doing and our thinking, leaves us blank and forgetful in everyday empirical life. In just the same way there is no "essential" goodness that expresses itself in discordant action, just as there is no "essential" maturity that expresses itself in anything other than mature action.

There may of course be temporary impediments: for example, without any fault of his own, a man may become stunned, fogged by drink or drugged, just as he may pass through a crisis as the result of illness; but if his constitution and formation are reasonable solid, removal of the impediment or cessation of the pathological phenomenon will be sufficient for him to regain full possession of his faculties, to return to his normal state. And the memory forms an integral part of this state, for without it the other faculties could not function properly, nor could a man's other potentials and virtues be properly exercised.

It may well be that our subject returns to normality as if he were waking up from a long sleep, as if nothing had happened, but the loss of memory for the entire period during which he remains deprived of consciousness throws his whole being into crisis and involves all his other faculties, involves his behaviour and reaction at every level. Loss of memory implies impairment, disablement of the whole man, and can be tolerated only if it constitutes a temporary lack, a kind of sleep from which one can reawaken, when it forms part of an illness, malaise or injury from which one can recover, at the same time regaining full possession of one's memory.

To the extent which it is effectively recovered, regaining one's memory implies global recovery of the personality. Loss of memory, with its obnubilation of the past, can be a temporary fact deriving from pathological causes and even altogether normal phenomena, as we have already said; and only if it is a temporary fact can it avoid having an altogether decisive and strongly negative effect on the maturation of an individual; if it is permanent, indeed, it can even annul this maturation.

Moreover, the maturation attained by an individual is shown by the manner in which he expresses himself, the way in which he thinks and acts. Except for temporary crises due to factors that suddenly manifest themselves and originate outside the person, it is simply inconceivable for a man to be in real and substantial possession of a maturity that does not express itself in a corresponding maturity of thought and action or of anything else that may constitute the concrete counterpart of the presumed interior maturity.

Given a very small child, a newborn baby at the very beginning of its earthly existence, nobody could reasonably say that this creature has already substantially learnt many things (in the course of its previous lives, to be sure) when it is quite obvious that the baby has to start literally from scratch with everything that has to be learnt. One may say that the child's organism can already function perfectly in all its cells, but here we are concerned with a set of unconscious movements that the body can perform right from the beginning, movements that already contain all the forerunners, the patterns of the movements that will later correspond to growth and development, just as the pattern of the structure and the unconscious behaviour of the entire organism is already contained in its germinal cell. But all this has nothing whatever to do with learning, at least the kind of learning with which pedagogy and didactics are concerned: learning is something that passes through consciousness, develops at the level of consciousness and, even though it may become filed or stored in the memory (which is unconscious), it proves effective only if the information enclosed in the compartments of the memory can, on command, be brought back to the level of consciousness and thus be made available for further processing; even though this processing does not always and not wholly take place at the level and in the light of full consciousness, it is yet the person's consciousness that sets this process in motion, that sanctions it as it were.

A child is born with attitudes, dispositions and tendencies that, submitted to our judgment, will be considered either positive or negative, there is no reason why one should not suppose that these tendencies derive not only from the structure of the germinal cells with which the parents have conceived the child, but also from the astral residues that have become reincarnated in him after having been left behind by disincarnate souls in their ascent to a higher and subtler vibrational level. But all this explains only the origin of the child's dispositions, attitudes, tendencies, and potentials. Applied specifically to learning, we could say that it explains the *capacity* (or otherwise) of learning certain things more or less easily, more or less thoroughly, in the course of a process of longer or shorter duration.

All this therefore concerns a *subject's capacity for learning* certain things, certainly *not* the fact *that he has already learnt them*; indeed, one could hardly say anything in greater contrast with our concept of learning than such a claim, one could hardly make a statement that would seem in greater conflict with our up-to-date and thoroughly pondered idea of what has to be understood by learning, fruit of the millennial travail of our philosophy, our science, and our pedagogic practice.

Personally I am very acutely conscious of having learnt what little I know gradually and in the course of a long series of experiences, and also as the result of processes of a more abstract, notional and mnemonic type. Taken as a whole, the process was – and still is – very toilsome. One is generally more inclined to waste a fortune one has inherited or won in a lottery, but one is far less ready to lose a patrimony, be it ever so modest, that one has succeeded in putting together as the result of long years of hard work. The very zeal and commitment one has dedicated to the accumulation of this wealth bears witness to the importance it had in the eyes of the person pursuing this goal.

And one can also readily understand the great difference between what one *has* and what one *is*. It may be that, notwithstanding a lifetime's work, one accepts comparatively readily that some day, on the occasion of death, one will have to abandon and leave behind *what one has*, but *what one is* should surely represent a far more precious treasure. It is true that our consumption-based industrial civilization does not place the accent on being rather than having, but there are still people who seek to be more. To be more does not mean merely to have a healthy, robust and beautiful body, and to be well dressed: it means, above all, having developed certain gifts of the soul that, presumably, will still constitute a treasure for the soul, safe from rust and weevils, even at a time when the body has been abandoned to the worms.

There is an ascetic tendency to place the accent, first and foremost, on ethical and religious values in the strict sense, cultivating the corresponding virtues in an exclusive manner. The important thing, as some people put it, is "to save the soul" rather than developing one's intellectual and creative faculties: the important thing is "to become holy" or, at least, "to be good"; in this way one can gain access to "paradise", where one will behold the "beatific vision of God" and, at the same time, have the perfection that represents a goal far loftier, indeed immeasurably more lofty, than any that humanism, however conceived, may ever have dreamt of setting itself. But the problem, surely, is also one of seeing whether humanism, culture, man's creativity and initiative, in organized form even, cannot in some way co-operate in the kingdom of God: not only to prepare it, but also to complete it.

In an approach of this kind, which would clearly seem to be less limited and therefore richer and more integrated than the other, everything we do to ensure the integral formation of our personality, i.e. an all-round formation rather than a mere ethico-religious one, is recognized as being of value, sometimes even of decisive value.

If man's end is the full realization of all the potential that is in him, pedagogy itself does not fail to tell us that man's formation is always and inevitably also *self*-formation: that is to say, no matter what part or aspect of formation is considered, it always calls for the active, creative collaboration of man himself. This means that man is called upon to collaborate even in the creation of paradise, in the creation of the kingdom of God, at least if we take "paradise" and "kingdom of God" to be two expressions that contribute to designating what should some day be the perfect condition of man.

I have indulged in this digression to motivate – amply, it would seem to me, discounting the brevity of my remarks – the great importance I attribute to the things I have learnt: the things I have learnt with a great deal of toil and which, taken as a whole and modest as they are, constitute what I could call my culture, the form and the degree of the maturity I have acquired, my interior world, my personality, my way of being if you like, what I have succeeded in making of myself, what I *am* as distinct from what I *have*, the things that presumably I shall take with me when I shall have to leave my exterior assets and even my physical body. It constitutes a modest *quid*, as I was saying, and, let me add right away, is full of gaps, full of defects, full of miseries, just as it contains many unpleasant memories. We have come to a point where our considerations become existential in the first person and therefore autobiographic, even though in general principle they can all be adapted to what any other person could say about himself in this context, in this type of reflection.

I am not always pleased with myself, and there are even many occasions when I should like to be somebody else and, consequently, be no longer bothered by this person that I am. Who, after all, can stand himself for 24 hours a day, 365 days a year? Who considers himself to be so wonderful? Who is really satisfied with himself? Certainly, not I; and anybody else, I believe, unless he be absolutely infatuated by his empirical ego in an abnormal and pathological manner. Nevertheless, it seems to me that I show myself far more respect, far greater esteem, when I see myself as a human subject, especially in a religious perspective like that of the Bible, where man does really seem to be made in the image and likeness of God, where he seems himself a god by virtue of his part in divine life and creation, a god who is beginning.

When I look at what I am at this moment, I can see myself on a rung that is probably very low and down-to-earth, and yet forms part of a ladder that has to take me very high up; even though it is a transcendental initiative that calls upon me to elevate myself and gives me the strength to do so, it is yet an initiative to which I must respond with my own initiative, with all my will and all my intelligence and creativity, with my own effective action, if I am to climb the rungs, one by one, right up to the top. And no matter how low the rung on which I am standing as of this moment, I yet feel that it represents a set of precious conquests.

I cannot therefore see anything positive, good or attractive in the prospect of losing all memory of the things I have learnt and forgetting even what I am. Among others, it would mean losing everything that constitutes my present maturity. It would mean *losing many acquisitions* and going back to possessing *a mere capacity for learning* these things all over again, *be it even better* than the one I had at the time I began my present life. But can I really accept the idea that, in exchange for nothing other than a better *potential*, I shall on each occasion lose something that for me already represents a *very real and concrete asset*, no matter how limited it may be?

My reluctance to forego the sum total of these modest accomplishments springs from my awareness of the value they represent for me. I could never consider these humanist accomplishments as nothing other than a *means* to attain even greater potentials; as far as I am concerned, they represent *a value in themselves*, a patrimony that, undoubtedly, I can and must keep on enlarging, but which I would never be prepared to throw to the winds, which simply is not available to be bartered or traded for something else.

In business, of course, one buys and sells, and a businessman is undoubtedly ready to sell many of the things he has in order to buy others that may represent even greater wealth, and sometimes even only potentially so; but I am convinced that even the most thick-skinned businessman has some things he is not prepared to sell, no matter how attractive the bargain may seem, because to his eyes they represent an absolute value. Here we have the problem in a nutshell: a reincarnationist is prepared to lose all memory of his empirical self, and to lose it once and for all, for the simple reason that his empirical self, his personality, does not represent an absolute value for him.

For a reincarnationist, even though his doctrine may be closely connected with a whole series of assumptions, the only absolute is the God whom he can find within himself, deep down in his own intimacy: but the God in question remains distinct and detached from the personality of the man in whom he reveals himself.

The kind of God that corresponds to Hindu, Yoga and Upanishad concepts, is not exactly a god who incarnates in man. The incarnations of Hinduism and mahayanic Buddhism are always incarnations of a god, or even of the absolute God himself, who assumes a human form, a human guise as it were, but does not become man in any effective sense: properly speaking, therefore, one cannot say that such a God assumes the totality of human nature, i.e. personal and empiric nature as well as corporeal nature, in order to deify it. The divine and the human remain distinct, two self-contained entities. The divine can have its privileged place of presence in man's interiority; the divine, again, can help whatever is divine in man to free itself from the empirically human, which latter is not assumed by the divine: consequently, the empirically human is not deified, but is simply left to itself and eventually thrown away like dross, as something that is negative and represents a non-value.

In the biblical tradition, in Jewish-Christian thought, on the other hand, the very marked creationism expressed there finds its ultimate perfection in an incarnationism that, likewise, is conceived and lived in the strongest sense, in a sense that is extremely real, concrete, and effective. It follows from this that an absolute value is assigned not only to the divine that is in man (considered as abstract and separate from the rest), but also (and specifically so) the human that is in man, the empirical, the singular, the personal, the bodily itself: the whole of man, man specifically as an individual personality, man as "this man here", is assumed by the divine, becomes divinified (at least potentially so on the basis of an ongoing process); and thus it is precisely man as an individual, with everything that this implies, to have absolute value, even though, rather than being originary, his absolute value is derived from the Absolute itself, i.e. from God.

It is my consciousness of all this that makes me unwilling to forego what little I am, for I know that it is an absolute. Moreover, even before attaining this clear awareness (and one can acquire it only as the result of a long travail of reflection), even before developing a wider line of thought in a metaphysico-religious perspective, I am conscious of all this in an intuitive manner, no matter how confused it may be. The idea of bartering what I actually am for some other asset or potential asset has always been repugnant to me, and this for the simple reason that I have always had the idea, albeit vague and confused, that I, as an individual, as an empirical personality, am an absolute that can neither be cancelled nor bartered by virtue of the fact that it merits absolute respect. Everybody, therefore, is worthy of absolute respect by mere virtue of being a human person, and this quite independently of whether he is a genius a hero, a saint, a benefactor or meritorious in some other way or, to go to the other extreme, a criminal or the most miserable and abject of individuals.

All this, which one can come to understand rationally or by mere intuition, also finds expression in the interest I take in others, in their personality as individuals, in the life of each one. Each one of us is a work of art that God begins to create, gradually overcoming the resistance of matter, with the intention that it should ultimately become his masterpiece. Each one of us is irreplaceable in his uniqueness. I feel this within myself, just as I feel it with regard to every other human being. The pain and sorrow I feel on account of the physical death of somebody is also an expression of my refusal to admit that this unique being can be cancelled or nullified. Our human limits prevent us from appreciating the unique and irreplaceable value of *each* of our peers, and it is quite normal that almost the totality of other people should leave us more or less indifferent; but when we become fond of somebody, when the person concerned is a member of our family or an intimate friend, we feel a profound repugnance at the idea that this person can become completely cancelled.

Personally I could add that the pain caused me by the disappearance of a very dear person receives basic comfort from the conviction – and even more so, I would say, from the feeling, the profound perception – that this person is not really "dead", but has simply made himself temporarily invisible to us.

The ultimate meaning of all this is indeed this feeling, this perception, the profound experience that what is of value in itself in man is not only the divine presence, and not even what so many people call "individuality" and which, using a Sanskrit term, we could also call *purusha*, i.e. the individuality that is today "incarnate" in John Smith and could subsequently become reincarnated in Mary Jones, and then again in Dick Walker, Harry Taylor, and so on (and not forgetting, of course, Pierre Dupont, Maria Rossi, Hans Müller, etc.). What I am really trying to make clear here is that what is ultimately valid in man also includes his personality, that is to say, the very fact that he is and always will be John Smith, a person that cannot be interchanged with another, singularly called upon to realize himself as an individual and in his own peculiar and irrepeatable manner, in a horizon of unlimited perfection. It is this very John Smith who represents the beginnings of a god, who is a god in embryo.

Each one of us can say of himself that he is such a John Smith having a unique personality, distinct from any and all others, with his own personal vocation and his own peculiar way of being, with a destiny of his own and unlimited prospects. The sense of the personality, of personal creativity, of everything that is unique in the human personality, has been greatly developed by modern thought and modern sensitivity, which have crystallized ideas that to a very large extent were already present, at least as germs or embryos, in the Jewish-Christian tradition in which these ideas have their roots.

For the most part modern thought aims in a secularizing direction and often tends to forget this Jewish-Christian root from which it springs. I am profoundly convinced that only by rediscovering this root will modern thought be able to reconstruct an absolute perspective for itself, and this is as true for modern thought as a whole as it is for all the elements from which it is made up. What, after all, would the person be in a purely mundane and earthly perspective in which all things are destined to perish? Were this person even the most extraordinary individual, rich in inner experience, knowledge and creative genius, a truly great man of action with untold achievements to his credit, what would he be if not a prisoner condemned to death ?

Only God, the Eternal, makes us immortal, saves us from the death that would otherwise be oblivion, the cancellation of everything we are, everything we do. All life within us would be destined to become arid, would exhaust itself and come to an end, if it did not receive continuous sustenance from this Source of life, from which we can draw the prospect of life without end.

The creationist vision of biblical tradition is that of a creation understood in the strongest sense of the term, a consistent and valid creation, not a phantomatic one (as it always is to some extent, at least tendentially so, in the Hindu view, no matter how interesting this may appear in many other respects). Only in the perspective of a divine creation in this strong sense can the things that we men create – and therefore also our humanism – have the ambition of representing an effective collaboration that we offer God to complete his own creative work. Only in the perspective of a divine creation in this strong sense can there really be for man, as also for his humanism, "words of everlasting life". Here therefore, and only here, do we have a perspective of eternity and infinite perfection for the personality of individual man, a perspective in which each one of us, following his own personal path, is on the way towards this absolute goal.

Only in the perspective of a divine creation in this strong sense does the creature receive an absolute convalidation, only in this perspective does it acquire absolute importance as an individual creature, with everything that constitutes its singularity, its ontological consistence as an individual, a single thing: here a stone, a tree, an animal, an individual man, and also every single work of man and every work of art, has a consistence *in se* and not merely because it is the expression or vehicle or symbolic figure of a transcendental metaphysical reality.

At this point I think I have said enough to convey the idea that this proclamation of the value of the individual, the single person, with a forcefulness that has neither precedents nor equal is the work of a tradition of culture and thought that has its essential roots in the spiritual tradition of creationist theism in the strong sense of Israel and the Bible. And it is in the stream of this tradition and its Christian fulfilment as well as its subsequent humanist developments, that the value of the personality of individual man is specifically affirmed as such: it is here that the reasons for this value appear in all their profundity, it is here that its implications are developed more than ever before.

It is true that a certain secularism tends to lose sight of the very thing that constitutes the ultimate root and meaning of all this: but it is a root that has to be rediscovered in order to highlight the original design, to integrate it. To develop modern humanism in all its implications, at the same time leading it back to its spiritual and metaphysico-religious roots, means bringing about the great synthesis that our time is beginning to feel as an ever clearer and more pressing need. Every civilization, every spiritual tradition, each in its own particular way, can make an essential contribution to this synthesis; and this is particularly true as regards the great and complex spiritual tradition of India.

It seems to me that the definition of the idea of the individual human personality in all its profundity and wealth is due, above all, to Christian spirituality, derived from Jewish spirituality and fertilized by contributions from the classical civilization, culture and philosophy, and subsequently further developed in many of its elements by that selfsame modern humanism that, even though such a large part of it has seemingly become forgetful of its deepest roots, will yet have to rediscover them sooner or later if it is to understand itself better, become integrated and completed, and attain to the fullness of its significance.

Let us for a moment consider this perspective of a Christianity developed in all its humanist implications or – what really amounts to the same thing – a humanism led back all the way to the Christian roots from which it sprang. And in this specific perspective let us imagine ourselves in the company of some man or woman, engaged in a conversation of a certain depth concerning our true being. Let us therefore imagine that we turn to this person to ask: "Who or what are you really?" Even if we were to attribute to this question every possible metaphysical significance, the answer "I am John Smith" or "I am Mary Jones", i.e. the fact of answering the question by simply declining one's name and surname, would be *only seemingly* a trite reply in a biblical or Christian perspective. In a certain Hindu perspective, on the other hand, "I am John Smith" would be equivalent to the most superficial of presentations (valid only at a purely empirical, social and anagraphical level), it certainly would be more meaningful in a biblico-Christian perspective, far more meaningful indeed.

In the Hindu view, especially if of a certain trend, "John Smith" is a pure appearance, just as individuality is an illusion that keeps men prisoners in our spiritual ignorance, our lack of discernment in connection with what we truly are in the depth of our being.

At the opposite end of the scale, in a traditional Judaico-Christian perspective, into which one can integrate also certain humanist views open to transcendence, being this particular individual – John Smith or Mary Jones, for example – is not only an empirical fact but also, and above all, a metaphysical one: here the personality of the individual is anything but purely evanescent appearance, it is the term of a creation in the strong sense that causes each man to be constituted as a strongly individualized spiritual, psychic and corporeal subject, rich in being and value and having an infinite potential, ontologically dense and autonomous in his relative "aseity" (i.e. his being relatively self-derived, i.e. the principle of himself) that imitates the absolute aseity of God and partakes of it.

This individual personality, though highly important in the spiritual tradition of our Western world, is not put into the limelight in a similar manner by other traditions, which concentrate their attention on other realities. For the purposes of knowledge, however, attention is undoubtedly a most important thing. It is very difficult to imagine that we can fully know and evaluate, gain thorough insight into something that we do not focus so as to place it at the centre of our attention, for we will simply not be interested in it. The reasons for this lack of interest can be quite readily explained in psychological terms, for anything that remains in the margins of our field of consciousness will gradually tend to become dimmer, so that it will eventually fall into oblivion and, in a certain sense, no longer exist for our eyes.

This is not the place for trying to analyze the historical reasons and the cultural and spiritual developments that led Indian thought to such a grave undervaluation of the world, of nature, matter and the creation in general, and also of time and history, of the individual, of the single person conceived as a personality. This is the negative counterpart of the positive discovery that in the intimacy of each man there is a point, a pure spiritual principle, that seems to coincide with or, at least, to participate intimately in the pure principle of the selfsame intimate life of God.

Man and God are abyssally different, for God transcends man to an infinite extent; and yet there is a point where God and man touch each other and almost coincide: this is the point where the purely human spiritual principle becomes one with the divine principle, where the *atman* seems to coincide with the *brahman* (or, at least, seems to communicate with it in the most intimate of manners). The Indian spirituality expressed in the Upanishads concentrates its attention on this point of the human spirit where it seems to coincide with the divine spirit or, at least, to touch it and to partake intimately of it; and everything else is relegated into the margins of attention, so that it ends up by remaining hidden in the shadows, seemingly devoid of influence, not valid, negative, something that one must seek to cast off in order to become identified exclusively with what stands at the centre of attention and is increasingly seen as the most important thing, indeed as the only important thing, as the sole reality, as the sole true being of man.

And that is why an Indian (or, for that matter, any person educated in the spirituality of the Upanishads) will have a ready and short answer to the question "Who or what are you really?", saying simply: the *atman*, namely the atman that is one with the *brahman* or, alternatively, has this extremely close relationship of participative identity with the brahman. And if he had any doubt in the matter, the *Chandogya Upanishad* would immediately come to his aid with the words that Uddalaka Aruni addresses to his son Svetaketu: There is a "subtle essence" in all things and "it is by virtue of this essence that all things are animated; it is the sole reality; it is the *atman;* and this is what you are, O Svetaketu".[223] Here we have the famous *tat tvam asi,* "this is what you are", that pinpoints our true being not in our personality as men (which is here conceived as something that is but superficial, ephemeral, and illusory), but rather in the atman, which is intimately related with the pure principle of every reality.

For Buddhism, again, all the realities are unstable, nothing is permanent, and any intrinsic and individual permanence is therefore altogether inconceivable: there is no such thing as an atman. A Buddhist, questioning himself about his own intimate essence, could never conclude, as Svetaketu does, "I am the atman". What, then, is it that, following the physical death of an individual, transmigrates into another body, into a person about to be born? No atman, certainly, no individual soul, but quite simply the *karman,* the fruit of one's actions, the sum of the positive and negative consequences of the actions committed or performed by the psychosomatic personality or personalities that previously carried or possessed this selfsame karma. Rigorously speaking, on being asked "Who or what are you?", a Buddhist should therefore answer: "If, notwithstanding the general impermanence of all things, I have to identify my true being with what is least ephemeral within me, I certainly cannot say that I am either my body (which is in continuous transmutation and dissolves upon death) or a presumed individual soul of mine (which is devoid of substance, reducing to a mutable and temporary aggregate of psychic-phenomena and therefore destined once again to dissolve as such); consequently, if I really have to identify myself with something within me that is relatively permanent, I cannot identify myself with anything other than my karma, that is to say, with the fruit of the actions that derives from my present personality and from previous and no longer existing personalities, a fruit that, upon the dissolution of my present personality, will gradually transmit itself to other personalities yet to come. In this particular perspective, indeed, rather than saying that man *has* a karma, one should really say "man *is* his karma."[224]

Primitive-archaic man, and especially primitive man, on the other hand, is at a complete loss to understand what sense there can be in the exquisitely ascetic preoccupation of severing all the links that can in some way involve the true I in the empirical realities or in some way and to some extent identify it with them. Indeed, the I of primitive man, in an altogether different manner, tends to extend in all directions and to embrace and include what scholars call his "appurtenances", all the things that belong to him. To the question "Who or what are you really?", therefore, primitive man could respond in a manner that, translated into our own language, would sound more or less like this: "I am all my appurtenances: I am my body, but also – and above all – my soul and my personal name (which I keep a secret, so that my enemies shall not get to know it and cannot therefore put a spell on it, which could harm me and, in the limit, even cause my death); in the same way I am my image (which I do not allow anybody to possess or take, with a photographic camera for example, for fear that somebody who bears me ill could obtain possession of it for the purpose of harming me by means of practices of black magic that, by acting negatively on my image, would end up by acting negatively also on me because, as I have already said, I am also my image); and in the same way I am my hair, even when it is cut (so that, for the same reason, I take care to destroy it or to make it disappear); but I am also my clothing, my arms, my home, all the things that belong to me; and I am also my sons, to whom I have given life and in whom my life survives and perpetuates itself, just as I am my parents and my forebears, whose life has been transmitted to me so that I, in turn, can transmit it to my sons and descendants; in the same way I am my tribe, I am like a cell of this collective body (so that any honour rendered to this appurtenance of mine is an honour rendered to me, just as an offence to the tribe is an injury inflicted on myself; and therefore I have to avenge this offence, I have to avenge the killing of a man of my tribe by, killing a man of the tribe to which the killer belongs)."

Quite apart from certain archaic and barbaric applications of this concept, applications that seem to re-evoke the archaic and barbaric atmosphere of more primitive stages in the development of mankind, one has to recognize that the essential idea behind it is anything but peregrine: it is simply the idea that every expression of life is communicated to others by following privileged channels that depend on the particular vital relationships that are or become constituted around the individual.

Parapsychology, for example, shows us that telepathy takes place far more readily when affective bonds deriving either from friendship or blood relationship exist between the people involved; further, as regards certain experiments commonly associated with psychometry, it is well known that clairvoyance is enormously facilitated when the sensitive medium can touch an object used (or formerly used) in the everyday life of the person (who may also be deceased) about whom it is desired to learn something via extrasensorial channels.

While primitive-archaic man is as a general rule more immersed in things and feels himself to participate more intensely in their intimate life, so that he does not succeed in distinguishing himself clearly and sharply from the things of the environment in which he lives and, above all, does not succeed in thinking of himself as abstracted from his appurtenances, in short, while primitive or archaic man feels himself more solidary with the realities that constitute his world, modern man is characterized by the very opposite attitude.

Here I have in mind, of course, the typical man living in organized form in our technological civilization, complete with his scientific and strongly intellectualistic mentality, with his life conditioned by the rhythms of production and consumption. Such a man is accustomed to objectivating and manipulating all the things around him, indeed, he does this even for the purposes of the cognitive process: he knows things in an intellectualistic and scientific manner, always beginning by establishing a certain distance between things and himself, the distance that makes possible objectivization, conceptualization, definition and exact measurement, logical deduction and calculation. This type of objectivating, intellectualistic and scientific attitude is tailor-made for grasping those aspects of things that lend themselves more readily to being objectivated, which in actual practice means the material aspects. If this type of knowledge does not find certain correction or compensation from a form of knowledge that is more intuitive and therefore capable of grasping the subtler and more spiritual aspects of reality, there will eventually arise a situation where man, accustomed to consider only matter, sees nothing but matter, convinces himself that there exists nothing but matter and that even man himself is a being made wholly and exclusively of matter, so that he is destined to dissolve wholly upon the death of his body. This man, enclosed as he is in his intellectualist-scientific mentality, will tend to identify himself with his body or, if you so prefer, with his psychosomatic organism, where the psyche may well be conceived as the vital aspect or principle that animates the body, but is not in any manner or wise conceived as capable of existing independently of the body or surviving its eventual disintegration.

In this markedly materialistic civilization of ours, however, one can still find many spiritualists, many people who believe in the survival of the soul, and also many people who experience this regularly or have experienced it on at least one occasion: these are subjects who, every now and again, have an *out-of-the-body experience* or have had such an experience at least once: these people, albeit in a manner that cannot be objectivated (though theirs is yet an existential experience, a first-hand experience), have had the experience of existing – in full possession of their faculties – outside the body, independently of the body, which at the time was lying somewhere, seemingly – at least in the greater part of cases – wholly inactive and devoid of life.[225]

These experiences of being to all intents and purposes a soul that can exist and function perfectly well without a body are confirmed and further deepened by the "frontier" experiences gone through by many people who, following some grave crisis of the organism, come close to death and are subsequently "brought back to life" in the resuscitation department of a hospital.[226]

Very well, then, let us put our question ("Who or what are you really?") first to the type of "modern man" with his intellectualistic-scientific and tendentially materialistic mentality we have just described, subsequently repeating it to the type of spiritualist still to be found even in a society like our own, who believes in survival on account of either the education he has received or his particular mental habits or because he has actually had an out-of-the-body experience. One would expect the first subject to identify himself with his body or – although in actual practice this amounts to the same thing – to identify himself with a more complex individuality, albeit even a psychic one, though still convinced that this dissolves completely at the moment of physical disgregation. Our second subject, on the other hand, can be expected to identify himself more specifically with the soul, which he will believe to survive the body or even to be immortal, capable of surviving forever, at the same time considering the body to be nothing other than a temporary instrument of that soul.

The question "Who or what are you really?" can therefore be

answered in many different ways. Let us very briefly repeat the essence of at least some of these possible answers: "I am this soul of mine, my psyche"; "I am this body of mine or, more precisely, I am something rather more complex, possibly even of a psychic nature, but this something forms an inseparable whole with the body, so much so that it dissolves completely on the occasion of physical death"; "I am not only my body and soul, but also all my appurtenances and participations"; "I am not exactly any of these things, I am neither my body nor my psyche, both of which are superficial, mutable and ephemeral elements, in the last resort I am only what within me is really intimate and truly stable, permanent and substantial, namely the *atman*, or – more precisely – I am the *atman* that forms a single whole with or participates in the *brahman*"; "Since there is nothing truly substantial and permanent, not even the atman, I am simply what is the most lasting and durable thing within me, namely the karma"; "I am my personality, that is to say, I am John Smith (or Mary Jones, Dick Taylor, etc.) constituted as such – not only empirically but also metaphysically – by the absolute itself, so that I, *specifically as an individual*, am constituted, at least potentially and in embryo, as a derived absolute".

As regards the last of these points of view or possible answers to our question, I should like to add a kind of postscript to bring out even more clearly that when – in the biblical perspective we have discussed – I affirm to be "John Smith", I do indeed distinguish myself from God (and in a truly infinite and abyssal manner), but at the same time I am saying that what makes me John Smith as a tiny and germinal absolute is a very particular divine presence within me: as a consequence of this, even though God transcends me in an abyssal manner, he is not exactly a "stranger" to me; quite the contrary, for in a certain sense He is more intimately me than I myself, He transcends me from deep within me as it were.

When looked at from this viewpoint, the idea that in the last resort I am the *atman* (which is one with the *brahman*) seems to be right on the mark and expresses a profound aspect of this reality. And this aspect has to be pin-pointed and underscored in all its importance, though certainly not in an abstract, unilateral or exclusive manner (as, unfortunately, is so often done). With respect to me, indeed, God is "totally other" in the sense that he transcends me in an absolute manner, but without for that reason being "another" in the sense of being a stranger to me. And therefore moral law, which once again comes to me from God, is never "heteronomous" in the sense that would have displeased Kant, it is never an obligation that is purely and simply imposed on me from outside. "A man by my side is another, an authority of the state is another," notes Romano Guardini in this connection, "but God is not 'another' in this same sense! . . . Obviously, He is not me. Between Him and me there is an immense abyss. But God is the Creator in whom I have the spring of my being and my existence; in whom I am more myself than I am within my very self. My religious relationship with God is wholly determined by this unique phenomenon that has no equivalent or counterpart elsewhere: the more thoroughly and profoundly I abandon myself to Him, the more fully I allow Him to penetrate into me, the greater the force with which He, the Creator, dominates within me, the more I become myself."(227)

I am my soul; I am my body; I am my appurtenances; I am the atman; I am the karma; I am my personality, in continuous and uninterrupted evolution, a tiny absolute in the making: all these affirmations, far from being contradictory, seem to integrate each other, seem to be complementary, in the sense that each statement places the accent on something that I really am.

How can I manage to be all these things at the same time? Is there not a contradiction here, does not one exclude the other? If I am one thing, how can I manage to be another at the same time? From a logical point of view, first of all, we may say that the logic of mutual exclusion applies only when the entities under consideration are determined in so precise and absolute a manner that each one of them *is* absolutely itself and *is not* absolutely other than itself: A *is* A, A *is not* Non-A, A *is not* B for the very simple reason that B is a Non-A. Consequently, when I say A, I exclude B; likewise, if I am A, for example, I cannot in any manner or wise be B at the same time. But where do we find beings determined with such accuracy and precision? We find them among the pure concepts and symbols of abstract logic and, again, among numbers, among geometric figures.

Considered from an abstract point of view, truth *is not* falsehood in as exact and absolute a manner as the beautiful *is not* ugly, and this quite apart from the fact that in actual reality we can find the beautiful and the ugly mixed in a rather intimate manner. Thus, two plus two is four and *is not equal to* five, and this in so absolute a manner that 2 + 2

= 5 is absolutely false, as absolutely false as the statement that 2 + 2 = 10,000,000. Thus, while it is absolutely true that the sum of the internal angles of a triangle is equal to 180°, to say that these angles add up to 181° is a falsehood, and in as absolute a manner, as saying that the degrees are 360 or zero. Similarly, a point that does *not* lie within a given geometric figure, a circle for example, and does not even lie on its circumference, must therefore lie outside it; it is therefore alien to it, does *not* lie within but outside it in an absolute manner, and this absoluteness is in no way dependent on the distance between the point and the circle.

In these things there never is a "more or less" and, once B has been defined as a Non-A in an absolutely exact sense, there never can be an A that at one and the same time is also a B. This applies quite rigorously to the ideal beings of logics and mathematics. But can one say the same thing as far as real beings are concerned? Are real beings as absolutely determinate and, consequently, as absolutely determinable? In actual practice the entities or beings of reality seem to become more and more compenetrant, they seem to participate in each other to an ever greater extent (and also in an ever more complex manner) as one rises from the level of inorganic matter (governed by the pure laws of physics and chemistry) to the various levels of biological, psychic and spiritual life. And it is precisely this mutual participation of two real beings A and B, this manner of participating in each other, that makes it impossible for A, certainly not in every respect but at least in some respects and via some privileged channel, to be at one and the same time also B.

Am I my environment? I am undoubtedly distinct from it, and yet I live in the midst of it, I breathe it, I nourish myself from it; and not only does the environment condition me at every moment, it also communicates itself to me, it makes me be what I am to the extent to which it becomes intimately a part of myself. And it is for this reason that I, who *am not* my environment, *am also* my environment.

I am my soul, and also my body, if it is true that a simple pinprick given me on the back of my right hand is perceived by me not as procured to something that belongs to me but rather as given to my very self.

But I am also my appurtenances, for these, too, in some way extend and prolong my body and my personality. As I mentioned before, parapsychology provides some important evidence to confirm this fact, of which primitive and archaic man has a particularly strong and vivid sense.[228]

A psychic can tell a great deal about me when he can keep my wristwatch or my ring in his hand, indeed any object that has been in close contact with my person and has maintained this contact for a considerable length of time. On touching this personal object of mine, the psychic identifies himself with it and, through it, eventually comes to identify himself with me: in this way, in fact, he can reach a state where he will feel everything concerning me as if he were living it in the first person, as if he had been transformed into me. Holding my ring in his hand, therefore, in a certain sense *the medium becomes my ring* and, through the participative mediation of my ring, he *also becomes me*; and this precisely because, in a certain sense, *I am also my ring*.[229]

As far as the karma is concerned, special attention paid to this fact, i.e. that in a participative sense I am not only my integral psychosomatic personality but also my appurtenances, can help me to understand better that, rather than *having* a karma I also *am* my karma. Following my physical death, my karma (i.e. the sum of the consequences that my past actions have produced within me, at that psychic level) becomes detached from the core of my surviving personality: it becomes detached together with the psychic residues that abandon this core and, following disgregation, can go to "reincarnate" in the personality of men living on this earth, guided in this by affinity. How then shall I speak of this process: shall I say that *something of me* has become reincarnated elsewhere, or shall I say that *I myself* have become reincarnated? On the basis of the above considerations, as my readers will readily realize, one would be perfectly authorized to put it either way, for ultimately there is no contradiction here at all.

As regards the fact that I am (among others) my own karma, I could pose myself the following question: if it is true that my karman will eventually become dispersed as a result of this reincarnation in other individuals who are and will be living on the earth after my death, should I desire to improve a karma that, following detachment, will no longer be mine? Even Guénon, who believes in the transmigration of psychic residues,[230] wonders why the ancients should have attached such great importance to the posthumous fate of the elements in question; and he then proceeds to explain this fact on psychologic grounds, recalling that ever since the dawn of prehistory men have shown a great deal of concern for the treatment to be accorded to their mortal remains (funeral rites, inhumations, etc.).

Quite apart from the question whether or not such funeral rites can really be of some benefit as regards the fate of the psychic residues, it remains a fact that many people do show a great deal of concern for their bodily remains *sic et simpliciter*, without it ever occurring to them that this could have any effect on the deceased spirit.[231]

The average reincarnationist desires that *he himself* should have been (in the past) this or that other person or persons, just as he looks forward (in future) to becoming such other persons: he is not in the least interested in either the past or the future of certain peripheral realities of his (a kind of clothing) that were not part of him in the past or will become completely detached from him in the future; in other words, he is not in the least concerned with who may have "worn" his present induments in the past or who may use them in future. It seems to me that here we have an attitude that can still be defined as egoistic.

Nor is there in this attitude the joy of receiving something as a gift from somebody else who used it before us; in just the same way it lacks the joy leaving something as a gift for others and thus, as it were, to continue living in this gift and in the future experiences of those who receive it.

Things are very different in the case of an authentic Buddhist: to the extent to which he will have succeeded in killing his egoism and enhancing his capacity for feeling himself alive in others, he will feel the joy of transmitting to others a positive karma and the sorrow of transmitting them a negative one, because he basically feels the life of these others as his own and the karma transmitted to them likewise as his own. We are here far removed from the exclusive preoccupation for one's "own" future reincarnation, which represents a wholly egoistic concern (even though it may have constituted the initial driving force behind the ascent of the spirit).

A reincarnation understood as transmigration of the psychic residues seems to be wholly in accord with the survival of the personality and its unlimited development *without solutions of continuity*, that is to say, without Sisyphus' absurd toil of going back and starting things all over again. Further, I believe that a reincarnation understood in this manner not only explains the phenomena of the reincarnation type and accepts the positive aspects of the reincarnation idea, but is also capable of reconciling them with the Jewish and Christian tradition.

Ultimately, however, all this aims at something that goes well beyond mere conciliation: the problem here is undoubtedly to put together various approaches, to compare them, and to see what could be the points of meeting and mutual integration, but the final objective is that of arriving at a perfectly unitary synthesis or, more precisely, an amalgamation of the Judaico-Christian tradition and modern humanism, a synthesis based on the peculiar and irreplaceable contributions of all the different traditions, especially that of the great spiritual tradition that is at home in India.

Notes

(1) I. Stevenson, *Cases of the Reincarnation Type*, Vol. III (Charlottesville, Va.: University Press of Virginia, 1980) p. 376.

(2) Ibid.

(3) Radhakrishnan, *Indian Philosophy* (London: George Allen & Unwin; New York: Humanities Press, 1966) Vol. I, p. 444. C. Humphreys remarks that, according to the Buddhist conception, "which reincarnates is not an immortal soul but the product of countless previous lives, a bundle of attributes called Character which is changing from moment to moment, and lacks any element of immortality which it could truthfully claim as its own" (*Karma and Rebirth*, John Murray, London 1943, p. 52). A. Di Nola points out that ancient Buddhism, at least in its purest form, excludes the existence of an individual soul (that is to say, of the atman of Brahmanic doctrines) and therefore considers inquiry into the characteristics of the soul to be a non-problem, so that there would seem to be neither mythological nor doctrinal justification for the transmigration motive (*Enciclopedia delle religioni,* in Italian, Vallecchi, Florence 1970-76, Vol. V, p. 1858, entry "Trasmigrazione"). Which I would take the liberty of commenting as follows: I entirely agree as regards the transmigration of a "somebody", but this would not seem to prejudice the possibility of the transmigration of a "something" in the sense I have already adumbrated and which, little by little, I shall endeavour to specify more clearly.

(4) Chapter XVII; quoted by Radhakrishnan, op. cit., p. 445.

(5) The *italics* are mine.

(6) "The Abhidhamma, says Mrs. Rhys Davids, adds nothing to the philosophy of primitive Buddhism; its raison d'être is the analytical,

logical and methodological elaboration of the existing materials . . . "
This is what we are told by La Vallée Poussin, who in his turn
concludes that "from the point of view of dogmatics, the
Abhidharmakosha, together with the *Bhasya*, is the book that affords
us the best knowledge of Buddhism (Low Vehicle)"
(*L'Abhidharmakosha de Vasubandhu* traduit et annoté par L. de la
Vallée Poussin, P. Geuthner, Paris, and J.-B. Istas, Louvain, 1926-31,
Introduction, pp. VIII and XII).

(7) *Samyutta* III, 22.

(8) See *Abhidharmakosha* III, 11 a-b. In a few words, there is a
"continuity without identity of individuality" (K. N. Jayatilleke,
Survival and Karma in Buddhist Perspective, Union Printing Works,
Kandy 1969, p. 2).

(9) Ibid., 17-18 a-d.

(10) Radhakrishnan, op. cit., p. 446.

(11) Ibid.

(12) D. Christie-Murray, *Reincarnation. Ancient Belief and Modern
Evidence* (London: David and Charles, 1981), p. 42.

(13) Summarizing the doctrine of the "Anatta", i.e. of the state of
absence of the soul as professed by Theravada Buddhism, Francis
Story concludes that what is produced in rebirth is "another being" that
is no longer me, no matter how much I may consider it continuous with
me and as something that has sprung from me: this is not a case of a
"soul" that enters an embryo, but rather the natural formation of a new
fetus modelled by an outside energy, sustained by the creative causal
impulse of some being that had already lived previously. Reporting
these conclusions reached by Story, Joseph Head and S. L. Cranston
note that these concepts of Theravadist scholars, which they judge in a
negative light, have little or no effect on the masses. In this respect the
two authors quote Alan Watts' observation to the effect that the great
majority of Asiatic Buddhists continues to believe reincarnation to be a
real fact, understanding it in the sense that what is reborn is a concrete
individuality (cfr. F. Story, *The Case for Rebirth*, Buddhist Publication
Society, Kandy 1959, pp. 9-11, 13; A. Watts, *Psychotherapy, East and
West*, Mentor, New York 1963, p. 49; J. Head - S. L. Cranston,
Reincarnation, The Phoenix Fire Mistery, Crown Publishers, New
York 1977, "Buddhism".

(14) "The statements about the operations of karma are made by the Buddha on the basis of inference based on clairvoyant observation" (K. N. Jayatilleke, op. cit., p. 21).

(15) *Brhad-aranyaka-upanishad*, IV, IV, 1-3.

(16) K. Walli, *Theory of Karman in Indian Thought* (Varanasi: Bharata Manisha, 1977).

(17) Ibid., p. 21.

(18) Ibid., p. 3.

(19) See K. E. Muller, *Reincarnation Based on Facts* (London: Psychic Press, 1970), p. 13.

(20) See ibid., p. 140.

(21) M. Bernstein, *The Search for Bridey Murphy* (Garden City, N.Y.: Doubleday, 1965), p. 36.

(22) T. Dethlefsen, *Das Leben nach dem Leben, Gespräche mit Wiedergeborenen* (München: C. Bertelsmann Verlag, 1974), "Age Regression".

(23) M. Bernstein, op. cit., p. 118.

(24) Ibid., p. 119.

(25) Ibid., pp. 121-122.

(26) Ibid., p. 122.

(27) T. Dethlefsen, ibid.

(28) Ibid.

(29) Ibid.

(30) T. Dethlefsen, *Das Erlebnis der Wiedergeburt, Heilung durch Reinkarnation* (München: C. Bertelsmann Verlag, 1976).

(31) Ibid., p. 43.

(32) "From the *O.K.* Club, a Democratic organization supporting (1840) President Van Buren for re-election, from Old Kinderhook, N.Y., his birthplace. See *Saturday Review of Literature*, July 19, 1941" (*Webster's New Collegiate Dictionary*, entry "O.K."). See Dethlefsen, *Das Erlebnis . . . , p. 163.

(33) T. Dethlefsen, *Das Erlebnis . . . , pp. 219-247.

(34) Ibid., p. 45.

(35) F. Lenz, *Lifetimes, True Accounts of Reincarnation* (New York: Fawcett Crest Books, 1980).

(36) I. Wilson, *Reincarnation? The Claims Investigated* (Harmondsworth, Middlesex, England: Penguin Books, 1982) p. 66.

(37) See ibid., p. 71.

(38) See Stevenson, *Cases of the Reincarnation Type*, op. cit., pp. 3-4.

(39) See I. Wilson, op. cit., pp. 86-87.

(40) Remembering that Edgar Cayce did not hypnotize but, under hypnosis, "read" in the past and future situation of the subject, it may not be out of place here to point out that even the previous incarnation of the subjects of this famous American sensitive generally conformed to a very particular pattern that can be traced back to Cayce's personal "culture": Atlantis, Egypt, Rome, the Crusades, the France of Louis XIV, XV or XVI, the American Civil War and a few others, intermingled with the usual commonplaces taken from "historical" films and novels and from the most topical parts of the well known theosophist esoteric repertoire (cfr. G. Cerminara, *Many Mansions*, Sloane, New York 1950).

(41) See I. Wilson, op. cit., pp. 88-89.

(42) See ibid., pp. 90-91.

(43) See ibid., pp. 91-93.

(44) See ibid., pp. 94-95.

(45) See ibid., pp. 113-119.

(46) See ibid., p. 112.

(47) See ibid., pp. 58-59.

(48) See ibid., pp. 156-159.

(49) See F. W. H. Myers, *Human Personality and its Survival of Bodily Death* (London: Longmans, 1903), chapter III. Cfr. also S. Voronoff, *Du crétin au génie*, Editions de la Maison Française, New York 1941, ch. III-VII.

(50) E. Servadio, entry "Personalità alternanti" in *L'uomo e l'ignoto, Enciclopedia di parapsicologia e dell'insolito* by U. Dèttore, Edit. (Milano: Armenia, 1978-79), p. 914.

(51) See I. Wilson, op. cit., pp. 122-130.

(52) I. Wilson, op. cit., pp. 137-138.

(53) Ibid., p. 139.

(54) See ibid., pp. 141-143.

(55) See ibid., pp. 106 and 143.

(56) See ibid., p. 145.

(57) See ibid., p. 147.

(58) See ibid., pp. 147-151.

(59) E. Fiore, *You Have Been Here Before, A Psychologist Looks at Past Lives* (New York: Ballantine Books, 1979), p. 45; F. Lenz, op. cit., p. 15.

(60) T. Dethlefsen, *Das Erlebnis* . . . , p. 14.

(61) H. Wambach, *Life before Life* (New York: Bantam Books, 1979), p. 177. See also the same author's *Reliving Past Lives: the Evidence under Hypnosis* (New York: Harper and Row, 1978).

(62) T. Dethlefsen, *Das Erlebnis* . . . , p. 56.

(63) See ibid., pp. 13-14.

(64) Ibid., p. 115.

(65) Ibid., p. 116.

(66) M. Bernstein, op. cit., pp. 121-122.

(67) Ibid., p. 145.

(68) H. Wambach, op. cit., p. 17.

(69) Ibid.

(70) Ibid., p. 18.

(71) T. Dethlefsen, *Das Erlebnis* . . . , p. 169.

(72) E. Fiore, op. cit., p. 79.

(73) T. Dethlefsen, *Das Erlebnis* . . . , p. 48.

(74) S. Edmunds, *The Psychic Power of Hypnosis, Paranormal Abilities and the Hypnotic State* (Wellingborough, Northamptonshire: The Aquarian Press, 1982) p. 74.

(75) I. Stevenson, *Twenty Cases Suggestive of Reincarnation* (Charlottesville: University Press of Virginia, 1974), published for the first time in 1966 as vol. XXVI of the *Proceedings of the American Society for Psychical Research.*

(76) I. Stevenson, *Cases of the Reincarnation Type* (Charlottesville: University Press of Virginia): Vol. I (1975) *Ten Cases in India*; Vol. II (1977) *Ten Cases in Sri Lanka;* Vol. III (1980) *Twelve Cases in Lebanon and Turkey;* Vol. IV (1983) *Twelve Cases in Thailand and Burma.*

(77) K. E. Muller, *Reincarnation Based on Facts* (London: Psychic Press, 1970).

(78) Ibid., §§ 9-15 (pp. 39-82).

(79) See ibid., p. 75.

(80) See ibid., §§ 16-25 (pp. 83-132).

(81) See ibid., p. 117.

(82) See ibid., § 22 (pp. 121-125).

(83) See ibid., § 23 (pp. 126-128).

(84) See ibid., § 24 (pp. 128-129).

(85) See ibid., p. 130.

(86) See ibid., p. 131.

(87) See ibid., §§ 32-37 (pp. 155-183).

(88) See ibid., p. 40.

(89) See ibid., p. 42.

(90) See I. Stevenson, *Twenty Cases Suggestive of Reincarnation* (1974), pp. 19-34.

(91) Ibid., p. 31.

(92) Ibid., p. 32.

(93) See ibid., pp. 34-52.

(94) See ibid., pp. 52-67.

(95) See ibid., pp. 67-91.

(96) See ibid., pp. 91-105.

(97) See ibid., pp. 326-327 (Tabulation: Duration of Imagined Memories and Personation).

(98) See ibid., pp. 131-149.

(99) See ibid., pp. 203-215.

(100) Ibid., p. 240; see pp. 231-241.

(101) See ibid., pp. 274-305.

(102) Ibid., p. 383.

(103) Ibid.

(104) Ibid.

(105) See I. Wilson, op. cit., pp. 40-55.

(106) See I. Wilson, op.cit., pp. 49-50, and *Mind out of Time?* (London: Gollancz, 1981), pp. 56-57; A. Gauld, *Mediumship and Survival, A Century of Investigations* (London: Granada Publishing, 1982), p. 182.

(107) S. Giordani - L. Locatelli, *L'uomo e la magia* (Torino: S.E.I., 1974) pp. 229-230. This, be it clear, is a book of vulgarisation and written in journalistic style.

(108) H. Guimarães Andrade, *Um caso que sugere reencarnação: Simone X Angelina,* (São Paulo: Instituto Brasileiro de Pesquisas Psicobiofisicas, 1979).

(109) See ibid., p. 51.

(110) Ibid., pp. 50-51.

(111) H. Guimarães Andrade, *Um caso que sugere reencarnação: Jacira X Ronaldo* (São Paulo: Instituto Brasileiro de Pesquisas Psicobiofisicas, 1980).

(112) A. Gauld, op. cit., p. 174.

(113) Ibid., p. 187.

(114) See K. E. Muller, op.cit., p. 59.

(115) See I. Stevenson, *Twenty Cases* . . . , p. 16.

(116) See K. E. Muller, op.cit., p. 208.

(117) U. Dèttore, *L'altro Regno, Enciclopedia di metapsichica, di parapsicologia e di spiritismo* (Milano: Bompiani, 1973), entry "Ossessione".

(118) K. E. Muller, op.cit., p. 208.

(119) C. Balducci, *La possessione diabolica* (Roma: Edizioni Mediterranee, 1974), p. 16. See also the same author's *Gli indemoniati* (Roma: Coletti, 1959).

(120) Ibid., pp. 17-46.

(121) Ibid., pp. 47-70.

(122) Ibid., pp. 71-94.

(123) P. Sutter, *Il diavolo, Le sue parole, i suoi atti nei due indemoniati di Illfurt, Alsazia, secondo documenti storici* (Torino, 1935), pp. 150-151. The passage is quoted by Balducci on p. 91 of *La possessione diabolica.*

(124) See E. W. Stevens, *The Watseka Wonder* (Chicago: Religio-Philosophical Publishing House, 1887); D. St. Clair, *Watseka* (Chicago: Playboy Press, 1977). The first of these is almost unobtainable, while the second, though written in the form of fiction, gives an accurate account.

(125) See op. cit., p. 194.

(126) See I. Stevenson and S. Pasricha, "A Preliminary Report on an Unusual Case of the Reincarnation Type with Xenoglossy", *Journal of the American Society for Psychical Research*, Vol. LXXIV, 1980, pp. 331-348.

(127) E. Bozzano, *Indagini sulle manifestazioni supernormali* (Città della Pieve, Italy: Tipografia "Dante"), Vol. VI (1940), pp. 101-132 (Study entitled "Di un caso interessante di 'possessione medianica' [caso di Catanzaro]").

(128) Ibid., p. 109

(129) C. A. Wickland, *Thirty Years among the Dead* (Los Angeles: National Psychological Institute, 1924).

(130) Ibid., p. 72.

(131) See ibid., p. 23.

(132) E. Bozzano, *Dei fenomeni di ossessione e possessione* (Roma: Luce e ombra, 1926), p. 30.

(133) Ibid., p. 29.

(134) D. H. Buckley, *Spirit Communication* (Los Angeles: Sherbourne Press, 1967).

(135) H. Sherman, *The Dead are Alive! They Can and Do Communicate with You* (Amherst, Wisconsin: Amherst Press, 1981) p. 284.

(136) Ibid.

(137) See E. Bozzano, *Dei fenomeni di ossessione e possessione*, op. cit., pp. 5-6. A very long and extremely detailed report of the Thompson-Gifford case has been given by J. H. Hyslop (see "A Case of Veridical Hallucinations", *Proceedings of the American Society for Psychical Research*, 1909, 3, pp. 1-469).

(138) H. N. Banerjee, *The Once and Future Life* (New York: Dell Publishing Co., 1979), pp. 53-60.

(139) See I. Stevenson, *Twenty Cases* . . . , p. 61.

(140) Ibid., p. 52.

(141) Ibid., p. 59.

(142) F. Lenz, op. cit., pp. 71-73.

(143) T. Dethlefsen, *Das Erlebnis* . . . , p. 14.

(144) K. E. Muller, op. cit., p. 162.

(145) Ibid., p. 77. The author draws this last information out from p. 15 of a book by George B. Brownell, *Reincarnation*, Santa Barbara, Ca. 1946-49.

(146) See K. E. Muller, op. cit., p. 25.

(147) Ibid., p. 47.

(148) See ibid., pp. 122-124.

(149) I. Stevenson, *Twenty Cases* . . . , Note 29 of Chapter VIII (p. 346).

(150) R. Guénon, *L'erreur spirite* (Paris: Rivière, 1923) p. 208.

(151) One of the things that leaves me perplexed, for example, is Guénon's statement to the effect that memory depends on the bodily state to such an extent that "that there would obviously be no reason for it to subsist" after the death of the body (ibid., p. 208). To me, indeed, there is nothing "obvious" even in his other and equally drastic statement to the effect "that no authentic traditional doctrine has ever spoken of reincarnation, and that this is nothing other than an entirely modern and entirely Western invention" (ibid., p. 199). Faced with propositions of this type, which the author does not deign to justify in any way (not even with a reference to any of his other writings), even a confirmed antireincarnationist would be left with a great and unsatisfied curiosity. The reference that Guénon makes to early nineteenth century socialists, Kardechian spiritists and theosophers (or

theosophists, as he prefers to call them), on the other hand, seems intended to explain that modern reincarnationism is greatly inspired by the idea of "evolution"; an idea that is alien to the most ancient tradition, but is dominant in the nineteenth century (Lamarck, Darwin, etc.). In this connection see Chapters VI and VII of R. Guénon, *L'erreur spirite*, op. cit., as well as Chapter IV of the same author's *Introduction générale à l'étude des doctrines hindoues* (Rivière, Paris 1921) and Chapter XI of his *Le théosophisme, histoire d'une pseudoreligion* (Nouvelle Librairie Nationale, Paris 1921).

(152) R. Guénon, *L'erreur spirite*, p. 209.

(153) Ibid., p. 210.

(154) E. Servadio, "Natura e modalità della 'Reincarnazione'", *Luce e ombra*, LXXXII, 1982, pp. 235-236. In *"Reincarnazione e pseudoproblemi"* (Reincarnation and Pseudoproblems) (ibid., pp. 345-348) Giorgio di Simone, likewise, rejects any kind of identification of the permanent *quid* (the "individuality") with the empirical, exterior, relative and finite "personality". As far as individuality is concerned, the personality is a simple instrument, a "probe", an "antenna", that enables the quid to make certain essential experiences. The quid gradually evolves, while each empirical personality of which it avails itself is reduced to performing a purely instrumental function and is destined to dissolve upon physical death. The implications of this do not seem to me to be particularly comforting. If I am what I feel to be, that *alter ego* of which I know nothing (and, what is more, of which I experience nothing) would seem to be something wholly estranged from me and, at least for the moment, I simply fail to see the reason why I should be reduced to being a mere instrument of this other that absolutely has no meaning for me. Shall I succeed, sooner or later, in identifying myself with him? "Life will show" one may say, or – as seems more appropriate in this particular case – "Death will show". For the moment, however, the question seems far too abstract to have any vital, existential meaning for me. I quite admit that this may well be due to my own limitations. But then, is it really a limitation that I should be unable to resign myself, that I should feel this need of having for myself (and, indeed, for each and every one of us) something more, a great deal more? But at this point an objection comes to my mind: "Is it not that in a theist religious experience, like the one that is expressed in the Bible for example, God desired *everything* of us? Is it not that

He wants a total oblation?" Yes, indeed, He asks everything of us, but only to give us all. To give us all also at the empirical level. And of this 'all' that has been promised to us we already receive, if I may borrow the words used by Saint Paul, some 'first fruits' or 'earnest', a pledge of things to come, during this present experience of empirical life. And this ensures that this final and total realization of the gift will have a meaning for us even now: for we have the foretaste of the more limited realizations that, though incomparably more modest, we can already achieve as of this moment.

(155) Ibid., p. 236.

(156) R. Bayer, "La Reincarnazione", in *Metapsichica,* XXVIII, 1973, p. 139 (in Italian): "Is it not true that the communications with the world of spirits in which the greater part of our fellow spiritualists shows such a particular interest have hitherto been far from convincing and not therefore capable of proving Survival? Consequently, let say so once more, it is only through the phenomenon of Reincarnation that we can demonstrate our existence after the death of the physical body." See also, more generally, the entire article, pp. 136-139.

(157) The words inside the quotation marks constitute the well-known Cartesian definition of "substance" (see R. Descartes, *Principia Philosophiae*, I, 51).

(158) E. Servadio, op. cit., p. 238.

(159) Ibid., p. 239.

(160) I. Stevenson, *Cases . . . ,* Vol. III, p. 376. The *italics* are mine.

(161) E. Servadio, "Ancora in tema di reincarnazione", *Luce e ombra,* LXXXIII, 1983, p. 62. This note was written to answer criticism that Cobaltina Morrone (ibid., LXXXII, 1982, pp. 360-364) has levelled against Servadio's previously quoted article "Natura e modalità della 'Reincarnazione'" (see Note 154).

(162) A. Besant, *Death – and after?* Theosophical Manuals, No. III (London and Benares: Theosophical Publishing Society, 1901).

(163) Ibid., pp. 42-43.

(164) Ibid., p. 40.

(165) See A. D'Assier, *Essai sur l'humanité posthume et le spiritisme par un positiviste* (Paris: Pedone-Lauriel, 1883).

(166) E. Bozzano, *I morti ritornano* (Verona: Casa editrice "Europa", 1946), pp. 18-19.

(167) See E. Servadio, "Natura . . . ", pp. 238-239.

(168) D. Kelsey, "Reincarnation and Psychotherapy", in the book written by Kelsey in collaboration with his wife J. Grant, *Many Lifetimes: A Book about Reincarnation,* Doubleday, Garden City, New York 1967. The *italics* are mine. Apart from this aspect, which seems to me to be particularly interesting in the manner in which it is developed by Ugo Dèttore, the book seems to be really worthy of being considered "a fantasmagoria of psychedelic inanities", a kind of novel written in autobiographic terms, as it is castigated by A. H. Wagner in a note entitled "Reincarnation" and published in the *International Journal of Parapsychology,* X, 1968, p. 289.

(169) U. Dèttore, entry "Personalità regressive", *L'uomo e l'ignoto,* op. cit., p. 918. The *italics* are mine.

(170) See J. Roberts, *The Afterdeath Journal of an American Philosopher* (Englewood Cliffs, New Jersey: Prentice-Hall, 1978) p. 111. Ideas that, albeit in different ways, lend further support to my view of reincarnation can also be found in other well known mediumistic communications. For example: "I can only remember my life on earth, and that not very well, but I have a feeling that I existed before that. Sometimes the feeling is quite strong. It connects me with eastern lands. When on earth I felt drawn to eastern art and life. I still feel as if there were a link. I can't tell for certain, and it does not matter – besides, it is only a bit of me. Could *parts* of us have been in existence elsewhere?" (*From Four who are Dead, Messages to C. A. Dawson Scott,* Arrowsmith, London 1926, p. 138). A more precise interpretation is given us by the entity "Julia": "If you could imagine a wheel with many spokes, and each spoke capable of being detached and heated to white heat, and hammered on an anvil until it was fit to take its place in the perfect wheel, you can form some idea of reincarnation. There is not any total plunge into matter again, or ever. The Ego always has its vital principle on this side. The hub of the wheel is here, but the spoke is incarnate." (*After Death, A Personal Narrative, New and Enlarged Edition of "Letters from Julia," Amanuensis W. T. Stead,* Stead's Publishing House, London 1921, p. 149).

(171) Ibid., p. 7. See also p. 10 and more generally Introduction, 2 (pp. 6-11).

(172) J. A. Findlay, *On the Edge of the Etheric* (London: Psychic Press, 1977).

(173) Ibid., p. 134.

(174) Ibid., pp. 135-136.

(175) Ibid., p. 136.

(176) Ibid., p. 178.

(177) Cerchio Firenze 77, *Dai mondi invisibili* (Roma: Edizioni Mediterranee, 1977), p. 145.

(178) E. Barker, *Letters from a Living Dead Man* (London: William Rider, 1914), p. 98.

(179) See E. Bozzano, *La crisi della morte nelle descrizioni dei defunti comunicanti* (Milano: Bocca, 1952), p. 145.

(180) E. Barker, op. cit., p. 66.

(181) G. Cummins, *The Road to Immortality* (London: Ivor Nicholson and Watson, 1932), p. 123.

(182) Ibid.

(183) See K. E. Muller, op. cit., pp. 193, 198, 203, 207; § 41.

(184) See E. Bozzano, *La crisi della morte*, op. cit., p. 219.

(185) G. di Simone, entry "Spiritismo", *L'uomo e l'ignoto*, p. 1205.

(186) Ibid.

(187) E. Bozzano, *La crisi* . . . , p. 220-221. The *italics* are mine.

(188) J. A. Findlay, op. cit., p. 139.

(189) E. Barker, op. cit., p. 61.

(190) Ibid., p. 39.

(191) G. di Simone, *Rapporto dalla Dimensione X, La vita, la morte, l'aldilà* (Roma: Edizioni Mediterranee, 1973); *Il Cristo vero, Realtà del Cristo oltre il mito dei Vangeli* (Roma: Ed. Mediterranee, 1975); *Dialoghi con la Dimensione X. Oltre la morte* (Roma: Ed. Mediterranee, 1981). Cfr. E. Bianco, "La medianità ad incorporazione e l'Entità A," *Luce e ombra*, LXXXII, 1982, pp. 257-264; F. Liverziani, "L' 'Entità A': identikit culturale e connessi problemi," *Luce e ombra*, LXXXIII, 1983, pp. 139-146, and critique thereof by G. di Simone, ibid., pp. 147-151.

(192) G. Cummins, op. cit., p. 110.

(193) Ibid., p. 86.

(194) Ibid.

(195) G. di Simone, *Rapporto dalla Dimensione X*, p. 97.

(196) G. Cummins, op. cit., p. 82.

(197) Ibid., p. 83.

(198) Ibid.

(199) Ibid., p. 54.

(200) C. A. Dawson Scott, *From Four who are Dead, Messages to C. A. Dawson Scott* (London: Arrowsmith, 1926), pp. 44-45; quoted by E. Bozzano, *La crisi* . . . , p. 148.

(201) E. Bozzano, *La crisi* . . . , p. 91.

(202) Ibid., pp. 240-241.

(203) G. Cummins, op. cit., p. 67.

(204) See the fifth of the "fundamental particulars" in the conclusive chapter of this book, p. 301. See also G. Cummins, *The Road* . . . , pp. 80-81.

(205) E. Barker, op. cit., p. 39.

(206) Ibid., p. 37. The *italics* are mine.

(207) Ibid., p. 154.

(208) G. Cummins, op. cit., pp. 47-48.

(209) Ibid., p. 12.

(210) See D. Christie-Murray, op. cit., pp. 36-38 and 94-96.

(211) A. Di Nola, entry "Antenato", *Enciclopedia delle religioni*, op. cit., Vol. I, p. 411.

(212) See the depositions of Mother Agnes of Jesus, sister of the saint, in the ordinary canonical process and in the apostolical process. Cfr. *Manoscritti autobiografici di Santa Teresa di Gesù Bambino* (Milano: Editrice Ancora, 1958) pp. 332-333 (Appendice).

(213) E. Bozzano, *La crisi* . . . , p. 157; *From Four who are Dead, Messages to C. A. Dawson Scott*, op. cit., p. 182.

(214) Ibid.

(215) See G. Pagenstecher, *Aussersinnliche Wahrnehmung* (Halle:

Carl Marhold, 1924; *Die Geheimnisse der Psychometrie (oder Hellsehen in die Vergangenheit)* (Leipzig: Oswald Mutze, 1928).

(216) E. Bozzano, *La crisi* . . . , p. 157.

(217) G. Cummins, *Beyond Human Personality, Being a Detailed Description of the Future Life Purporting to Be Communicated by the Late F. W. H. Myers* (London: Ivor Nicholson & Watson, p. 76).

(218) Ibid., p. 77.

(219) Ibid., pp. 77-78.

(220) Ibid., p. 77.

(221) Ibid., p. 78.

(222) D. Alighieri, *Paradiso*, V, 41-42.

(223) *Chandogya-upanishad*, VI, VIII, 6-7.

(224) C. Humphreys, *Karma and Rebirth*, op. cit., p. 27: "Man *is* his Karma." The author quotes some verses by Edwin Arnold: "Karma – all that total of a soul / Which is the things it did, the thoughts it had / The 'Self' it wowe – with woof of viewless time / Crossed on the warp invisible of acts . . . "

(225) See E. Bozzano, *Dei fenomeni di bilocazione* (Città della Pieve, Italy: Tipografia "Dante", 1934); O. Fox, *Astral Projection, A Record of Out-of-the-Body Experiences* (Secaucus, N.J.: Citadel Press, 1962); C. Green, *Out-of-the-Body Experiences* (Oxford: Institute of Psychobiological Research, 1968); H. B. Greenhouse, *The Astral Journey* (Garden City, N.Y.: Doubleday, 1975); R. A. Monroe, *Journeys Out of the Body* (Garden City, N.Y.: Anchor Press, 1977); S. Muldoon - H. Carrington, *The Projection of the Astral Body* (London: Rider, 1929); D. Scott Rogo, *Leaving the Body, A Complete Guide to Astral Projection* (Englewood Cliffs, N.J., 1983).

(226) R. A. Moody Jr., *Life after Life* (New York: Bantam, 1976); *Reflections on Life after Life* (London: Corgi Books, 1977); M. B. Sabom, *Recollections of Death, A Medical Investigation* (New York: Harper & Row, 1982); P. Giovetti, *Qualcuno è tornato* (Milano: Armenia, 1981); F. Liverziani, *Le esperienze di confine e la vita dopo la morte* (Roma: Edizioni Mediterranee, 1986).

(227) R. Guardini, *La coscienza*, Italian translation (Brescia: La Morcelliana, 1948), pp. 58-59.

(228) See the Chapter II in *Les fonctions mentales dans les sociétés inférieures* by L. Lévy-Bruhl.

(229) See especially M. Inardi, *Dimensioni sconosciute* (Milano: Sugar, 1975) pp. 27-55, *et passim*.

(230) See the beginnings of Chapter V herein above.

(231) R. Guénon, *L'erreur spirite*, op. cit., pp. 209-210.